NEHRU'S
WORLD
VIEW

JAWAHARLAL NEHRU'S WORLD VIEW

A Theory of International Relations

By
WILLARD RANGE

UNIVERSITY OF
GEORGIA PRESS

ATHENS

To My Son
PETER

Publication of this book was aided by a grant from the Ford Foundation

PRINTED IN THE UNITED STATES OF AMERICA
BY FOOTE & DAVIES, INC., ATLANTA

Contents

Preface

THIS IS A CASE STUDY of Jawaharlal Nehru's theory of international relations. It attempts to describe his explanation of why states behave as they do and the reforms he is trying to bring about in the present inter-state system. Although some secondary sources have been used to ascertain Nehru's views, chief reliance has been placed on the considerable volume of his own expressions—speeches, books, interviews, press conferences, and articles—that have been increasing steadily in quantity for approximately forty years. The material for a detailed and definitive study will not be available, of course, until some years after Nehru's death. But enough material is available now to suggest the major lines of his thought; and that is what I have tried to describe.

My major interest is not in Nehru himself, however, despite the fact that he is one of the most fascinating people of our time. I am equally interested in anyone who is the manager of the foreign policy of a significant state. My major interest is in promoting my own and others' understanding of international relations; and understanding is likely to be deepened by a knowledge of the basic assumptions, theories, goals, interests, convictions, and what not that are in the heads of the practical politicians who make and execute the foreign policies of important states. Whether their ideas are unique or commonplace, crude or refined, gruesomely realistic or sublimely utopian they are important if they are in the heads of the men whose decisions significantly affect the behavior of states. It is by a study of the intellectual undercurrents in the minds of such leaders that we learn what they are trying to do and why they are trying to do it. Their diplomatic moves can be understood better by this depth-probing behind them. And once we have enough case studies of this type, it may be possible to do some generalizing about international relations that has not been possible hitherto.

I am not at all certain that I have done justice to Nehru at all points, despite my best efforts to understand his thinking. But Nehru has not made doing justice to him easy. With both the written and spoken word he has had tendencies to be so verbose and so vague that it is often difficult to cut through the flood of words and ambiguities to get at his meaning. What he seems to enjoy most in the way of expression is sheer intellectual rambling. He appears to have an aversion to speaking or writing systematically, as if moving from point to point in accordance with a prepared scheme would somehow cramp the impetuous and perpetual action of his mind.

But the effort to discover what has been going on in Nehru's head is rewarding. His mind is a provocative and stimulating one that has been working continually on public problems for over half a century; and some of his thought would be worth examining even were he not the important political leader he happens to be. He very definitely has a message for the world and it is a message worthy of the world's attention. His goal seems to be to adapt Gandhi's teachings to international relations; and although this has required much modifying, cutting, and re-fitting, the basic principles of the Gandhi philosophy are evident throughout.

Although political scientists are supposed to be still too ignorant to make predictions, I think it safe to risk a judicious guess that the Gandhi philosophy and technique of social change will continue to spread, and that there is considerable chance that they will have a powerful effect on international relations. A theory of international relations grounded upon Gandhi's thinking is therefore quite worthy of attention.

WILLARD RANGE

Political Science Department
University of Georgia

Chapter I

A New
Civilization

JAWAHARLAL NEHRU is a reformer who has been
driven throughout virtually all his seventy years by an almost insatiable urge to alleviate the misery of the masses of
mankind. It was from his father, he thinks, that he absorbed
his earliest tendencies to rebel against social customs and to
be aware of the wretchedness of most of his fellow men.
Then in England, where he went to study at the age of
fifteen, Nehru got interested in socialism and in the nineteenth-century European revolutions for freedom and democracy. The Irish movement for independence intrigued
him; and then he became impressed by the Russian Revolution even though at the time he knew almost nothing about
Marxism. He was simply concerned for the underdog, he has
asserted; and everywhere he went he saw that underdogs
made up the bulk of the population.[1]

Later when he read Marx a whole new way of looking at
history opened before him. It was not that he accepted Marx
uncritically. Far from it! Much that Marx had to say sounded
foolish to him; and the time was to come when Nehru was
to insist that Marxism as a comprehensive and systematic
philosophy of society was "out of date."[2] But the Marxist
perception of history as a struggle between the few who
owned property and the many who were propertyless tre-
mendously impressed Nehru and colored all his later think-

1

ing about history. It threw a white light on the exploitation he saw all around him and under which his own India was writhing.

When during one of his periods of imprisonment in the early thirties, therefore, he wrote a series of letters to his daughter that grew into a very respectable world history there was no doubt in Nehru's mind that history was essentially "the story of man's struggle for a living"; and he was in complete agreement with Marx that throughout the struggle whoever controlled the necessities of life, whoever owned the means of production and distribution, "lorded it over man." Throughout history the few had exploited the many.[3]

But although history had become to Nehru essentially the story of class struggle, it was not solely that. For Nehru saw also in history a strong urge in men to come together, to cooperate, and to work out their problems in common. Thus history was also the story of man's effort to learn how to cooperate with other men. He visualized the primitive single savage hunter and his family joining with other families to form a village, of villages coalescing into small states, and the cooperative urge then driving men into ever larger social groupings until at last the need and desire for global cooperation began to be expressed. It was through this cooperaton, thought Nehru, that man had progressed from barbarism to civilization; and he insisted that the degree to which a civilization had advanced could be measured by the degree of cooperation and sacrifice for the common good the people of that civilization had learned.[4]

Nehru apparently did not know at the time that there is no anthropological evidence to support this thesis. The evidence of anthropology is that social cooperation can appear and indeed has appeared in the most primitive societies and has been notably lacking in some matured societies. This means that cooperation is the result of conditioning and is by no means simply the result of an advanced stage of civilization. But Nehru's view was a popular one at the time.[5]

At any rate, as Nehru sat in prison devouring book after book about the past and reflecting on the course of history he felt forced to conclude that in both his struggle for a living and his effort to learn cooperation man had been largely a failure. Misery had remained the lot of most people and conflict had been incessant. What little progress had been achieved had come with painful slowness, and Nehru wondered many a time if the learning capacity of ants and bees was superior to that of man.[6]

Even in a period of renaissance, Nehru argued, when a civilization would rise to its greatest splendor, the masses of the people had remained wretched, penurious, and drab. The magnificent developments of a renaissance usually benefited only the few, and the struggle for a living by man was eased only a fraction.

Nehru agreed that periods of renaissance were wonderfully exhilarating interludes and that when they hit a people all society shot forward in all directions—economically, politically, socially, and religiously. People then became creative and energetic and all life became infused with a bubbling effervescence. The spirit of inquiry then spurred the mind and stimulated brilliant achievements in the arts, in government, and in all the realms of human imagination.[7]

But usually the renaissance was only an interlude. The age of glory would not last. The dynamism of the people was soon spent. Lethargy and indolence returned. Creativeness disappeared and the people again became imitators. Life decayed and became stagnant. Intellectually and spiritually people went back to sleep. Then instead of looking ahead and getting on the move they solaced themselves by dream-

ing of the glories of the past. They magnified and glorified
the past unduly and sighed for its return instead of driving
ahead to create a better and brighter future.[8]

Thus for thousands of years the great bulk of mankind
had remained in destitution, ignorance, ill health, and,
worst of all, it had remained exploited. It has been only in
the West and only in the past two or three centuries, according to Nehru, that substantial progress in the struggle for a
living has been noticeable. And it has been in the West too
that a sense of community responsibility and sacrifice for the
common good has been most highly developed. In the West,
indeed, at long last there has been some progress, thanks to
the spirit of science and inquiry that for some unexplained
reason persisted and even expanded there after the decline
of what to Westerners was *The Renaissance*.

But even the recent progress of the West has not greatly
alleviated the wretchedness of man, Nehru argued. Massive
problems of unemployment and poverty and of self-destruc-
tive wars on a colossal scale have continued to impose suffering everywhere. Thus it is vain and foolish even for
Westerners to boast of their great civilization. And such
problems are likely to continue until the West solves the
basic problems of life, until the West discovers and applies
principles essential to stability.[9]

Thus to Nehru virtually all history has been "unpleasant." The records of the past are steeped with evidence of
man's inhumanity to man. The exploitation of the many by
the few has been universal and perpetual. The vast bulk of
mankind has been enchained throughout the ages in a cess-
pool of ignorance, poverty, and ill-health. Conflict has been
unceasing. Man's behavior has been essentially selfish, irrational, impassioned; and his mind has been enslaved by
traditions, dogma, superstitions, and fear. For all his effort
to become civilized man has succeeded in lifting himself only
a few notches above the brutality and beastliness of the

lower animals. Thus life for the generality of mankind has been dark and grim, even the occasional brilliant periods of renaissance often being blighted by the tragedy of violent conflicts and by the horrors that grow out of even such a creative but intolerant movement as the Protestant Reformation.

Why all this should be so, why the past has been so "unpleasant" is one of the most puzzling questions Nehru has tried to answer. Hour after hour he has paced his prison cell "groping," as he calls it, for the solution of the riddle.

In this groping Nehru categorically rejected the theory that the "unpleasantness of history" was the result of imperfection in the nature of man. He is aware of the weaknesses inherent in man, as we shall see; but he does not agree that inherent human faults are responsible for man's misery. Nor has Nehru been willing to accept the explanation that human wretchedness is the result of "original sin"; for, as an agnostic, he has rejected out-of-hand the whole concept of sin. He has also virtually sneered at the so-called "devil" theory of history—the theory that holds that it is knaves who cause the world's troubles and that if men of sense and goodwill were placed in charge of public affairs the world's troubles would evaporate. For he insists that the men who run the world are not, with few exceptions, knaves. He argues that most of the leaders of mankind are equally as good as other men and that usually they manage affairs in the best possible way they know how to do so.[10]

Nehru's final answer to this problem, acquired obviously from the teachings of Gandhi and Marx, was that the "unpleasantness of history" was due to the systems or patterns of culture under which men have lived. He learned from Marx, for example, that the exploitation of man by man was the result of the types of economic systems under which men had lived, and he learned from Gandhi that the British treatment of India was due not to greed and cruelty in the nature of the British people but rather to the system of imperialism that dominated British culture. Thus India's quarrel was not with the British people or even with the British ruling class, but with the system of British imperialism. "I make no complaint of the English officials," Nehru once declared. "They are brave men serving their country to the best of their ability." Whatever injustice British officials imposed on Indians was dictated by the demands of colonialism.[11]

In like manner, Nehru refused to condemn the German and Japanese people for the horrors they were causing in the world in the thirties and forties, for it was the systems of fascism under which they lived that impelled them to behave as they did—"systems which deny freedom and are based on violence and aggression." Nor did Nehru blame the individual princes in India for the perpetuation of feudalism there. Some princes and their ministers were good and some were bad, he asserted; but whether they were good or bad was irrelevant, for the "evil lies in the system"—a system that had long since vanished from the rest of the world and would have vanished from India also had it not been propped up by British imperialism. By the same token, there was no point in blaming individuals who happened to be rich for their exploitation of the poor and the misery that exploitation produced, for so long as the economic system of society was based on exploitation the rich were merely fulfilling the economic function the system imposed upon them.[12]

In thus attributing the troubles of mankind to the cultural environment Nehru rejected outright both the pessimistic Machiavellian assumption that "all men are bad" and the optimistic or utopian assumption that "all men are good." Rather Nehru accepted the more modern conclusion widely held by nineteenth- and twentieth-century social scientists that man is born with a neutral nature—neither good nor bad—and that his behavior and attitudes are conditioned and determined by the cultural environment within which he is reared; and it is that cultural environment that must be changed if his behavior and attitudes are to be changed.

That a new civilization with new economic, social, and political systems is needed has long been one of Nehru's basic assumptions. Since the early thirties he has been arguing that the *laissez-faire* capitalistic system, the colonial system, the feudalistic systems prevalent in much of Africa, Asia, and Latin America, most religions and many other systems of contemporary civilization are out of date and no longer suited to the conditions of the twentieth century. Exploitation, poverty, and misery are today, he asserts, global problems that can be solved but the economic, social, and political systems dominant in much of the world were never designed to solve them. The whole structure of India needed to be revolutionized, for example, and Nehru had no patience with those Indians who believed that everything would be all right if the British ruling classes were simply replaced by Indian ruling classes. To him the whole Indian national movement has always been a movement aimed at revitalizing and changing all of India economically, socially, psychologically, and spiritually—not just politically. The entire cultural structure of his country needed to be modified to a significant degree and much of it needed to be discarded and replaced with something new—with systems based on equality, progress, science, cooperation, and freedom.[13]

The disappointing thing about World War II to Nehru was that the democracies showed no sign of fighting for a new order. Rather they fought to maintain the old out-worn order of the past. Before the war they had even appeased fascism—the bulwark of the old order—through fear that a new system like socialism would spread and deprive the

beneficiaries of the old order of some of their privileges.
When finally forced to fight in self-defense, the goal of the
democracies remained the restoration of the old structure
that had failed so dismally rather than the creation of something new. All that the leaders of the democracies were willing to do about a new civilization, thought Nehru, was pay
lip-service to some vague and better future. This was particularly true of Britain's wartime Prime Minister Winston
Churchill, declared Nehru, and even Franklin D. Roosevelt
had done little better.[14]

A year after the end of the war Nehru reiterated his
charge that the Allies had not fought the war to produce a
new civilization. Their goal all the time, he asserted, had
been merely to retain what they had and their leaders had
merely paid lip-service to democracy, peace, and freedom.
Indeed, by the end of 1946 Nehru saw the wartime allies
again preparing for a new war, and this was further evidence
that the peoples of the world had been betrayed.[15]

Yet even the apparent conduct of the Allies had not made
Nehru completely pessimistic about the possibility of a new
civilization; for he saw old systems everywhere decaying and
falling from their own weaknesses and a new society rising
from their debris. Toward the end of 1940 he asserted that
"present day civilization is ending and out of its ashes a new
civilization will be built up. . . ." Many forces were at work,
he asserted later, destroying old institutions and producing
new ones despite all the opposition being thrown against
them. A new constellation of Great Powers was appearing,
for example, out of the holocaust of World War II. The Soviet Union was destroying many relics of feudalism in both
Eastern and Western Europe. The industrial revolution, to
Nehru the greatest force in modern history, was also still at
work. It had been this industrial revolution, he declared,
that had produced the differences between East and West and
that had made it possible for the Occident to acquire as-

cendancy over the Orient. But now the industrial revolution was spreading to the remainder of the world and the inexorable changes wrought by it were bound to be momentous. Obviously it would produce a different kind of world, a new civilization wherein one part of the globe would no longer be able to exploit and dominate the other part. And to Nehru that was all to the good. The industrial revolution was also making it possible to abolish economies of scarcity and, for the first time in history, for mankind to produce enough material goods for all. The Soviet experiment with planning, which had long intrigued Nehru, also was spreading; and it too was powerful evidence that with the proper purpose and cooperation, all society could be changed, as it had been changed already even in extremely backward parts of Asiatic Russia. The pre-war type of capitalism, particularly the type emphasizing *laissez-faire,* was already in the process of disappearing, he thought. It was "a kind of luxury system for well-to-do nations," he declared. In the depression of the thirties it had revealed its inability to stand hard times and had already been abolished in many states. What was left would be greatly modified, he predicted, by greater planning and control.[16]

A vitally important part of the new civilization so urgently needed was, to Nehru, a new system of international relations. World War II, he asserted in 1939, was symbolic of the global crisis in which humanity then found itself, pulled as it was between the forces of imperialism on the one hand and democracy and freedom on the other. New forces such as elemental urges for freedom, food, and security were moving vast masses of people, he declared a year later, and history was being molded by the pressures of those forces. He wondered if powers like Great Britain would prove capable of adapting themselves to the new forces or if such nations would fall as past empires had fallen from inability to move and change with the inexorable course of events.[17]

When World War II was over and a new and better system of international relations failed to materialize Nehru was more than ever dissatisfied with the old system. In 1950 he told his Parliament that the current system of international relations, with its continued violence and wars, was vulgarizing people all over the world, making them brutal in thought and speech as well as in action. And he mused: "If this process continues, I wonder whether anything of value in life will remain for sensitive individuals." He charged at the same time that since World War II the foreign policies of most countries, based on the old system of power politics as they were, had failed more often than they had succeeded.[18]

International relations was no longer the old game of chess it had been once, he asserted in 1951 and later. A whole battery of new factors had arisen that made relations among states something quite different from what they had been formerly and that accentuated the need for a quite different interstate system. There was now, for example, a new weapons technology that threatened war on a hitherto unimagined scale and that made the whole international system of power politics out of date. There was now also the factor of mass aspirations. The foreign policies of governments all over the world were being determined by mass demands for food, clothing, housing, and health services for all. The technology capable of satisfying those demands was now available; and great hordes of people everywhere were determined that their needs be met. Thus international relations was no longer a game in which nations sided with one another in return for some territorial possession or similar gain; and a new system of interstate relations needed to be created that took account of these compelling factors.[19]

But how can a new civilization be created? How can a cultural environment be changed?

To this question there have long been a variety of answers. Nehru would be the first to answer, as we have seen, that all cultural environments are in a constant process of change resulting from normal economic, social, and political developments. Constant change, he has asserted, is a law of life and can no more be stopped than can the tides of the seas. Forces such as the industrial revolution are always at play in society; and even relatively stagnant cultures are continuously evolving, although ever too slowly. Feudalism, colonialism, and capitalism are among the contemporary systems being modified or destroyed in part at least by the normal course of events in modern history.

It is equally obvious to Nehru that social, political, and economic change can be achieved by conscious effort. Reform campaigns, revolutions, and wars have been the most common instruments of change throughout history. The major objection to these instruments, in Nehru's view, however, is that they are too often characterized by violence—usually physical violence—and that even non-violent reform campaigns are accompanied by one side gaining a victory over the other side; and of one side, therefore, suffering defeat and humiliation.

As a disciple of Gandhi, Nehru cannot help but prefer seeing modern civilization changed by non-violent methods —by the use of the Gandhian techniques of Satyagraha or something similar to Satyagraha. This does not mean that Nehru is willing to go as far as Gandhi in renouncing the use of violence. Throughout their association the two men differed on this point. But there is no doubt that Nehru has accepted the basic principles of Satyagraha as applicable to most situations and even believes that they could be applied to a considerable degree in order to achieve a transformation in the contemporary system of international relations. Nehru has never tired of telling the story of how Gandhi, by sheer talking, changed the attitudes and behavior of considerable numbers of the Indian people; of how by sheer teaching Gandhi dissolved people's attitudes of fear, strengthened their backbone, caused them to give up material possessions and to accept and even glory in suffering, and to apply goodwill and reason to the solution of problems. Then with their attitudes and behavior changed, they applied the technique of Satyagraha to change their social, economic, and political environment, which in turn produced even further change.

It is quite doubtful if Nehru ever had as much faith as Gandhi had in the capacity of man to be captain of his own soul. Once after reading a book on the French Revolution with all its horror and savagery, Nehru wondered if man's seeming inability to control his passions and elemental urges was conclusive evidence that man is a mere puppet of destiny without any control over his future.[20] But there seems to be an inherent optimism in Nehru's nature that refuses to let such pessimism linger for any length of time. The result seems to be that Nehru usually possesses great faith that the attitudes and behavior of men can be changed by conscious effort and that a new civilization, a different culture, a new set of economic, political, and social systems can be created.

Yet Nehru is not a utopian idealist living in an aura of optimism. There is indeed a great deal of pessimism in his world view. He knows that despite the rapid pace of modern change a new civilization is likely to evolve only with painful slowness. Most men are essentially conservative, he believes. They dislike and even fear change. Reformers, as Nehru avowedly is, therefore, can move society along at only a snail's pace. He is quite aware that progress can be made only to the degree one's fellow men are receptive to it and that receptivity is not easy to get. Nehru insists, in fact, that he does not even attempt to look very far ahead. Look-

ing into the distant future is the duty of professional philosophers, not the function of practical reformers like himself.
Rather he is concerned essentially with today's problems,
with merely the next step. And he knows quite well that
when one problem is solved another and often a more difficult problem takes its place. Thus the practical reformer
cannot afford to ignore the realities and limitations that
confine him, and brave words and gestures not in accord with
objective conditions get one nowhere.[21]

Nor is Nehru at all certain that the new civilization that is
unfolding all too slowly will be a better one than the civilization of the past. Many of the forces at work in the world,
particularly the forces promoting totalitarian dictatorship,
hold promise of nothing but unhappiness for mankind.
Even if the new civilization is better than those of the past,
moreover, it will not be perfect. So long as man lives there
will be problems. "It is the condition of life to have problems," Nehru has asserted. "Only the dead have no
problems."[22]

This all means, Nehru has declared repeatedly, that to be
an effective leader in public affairs one must also be a
compromiser. Ideals and principles there must be and a
good leader will always keep them in mind. A good leader
will always keep his high principles before him as a guide to
light the way. But in dealing with everyday problems that
demand immediate decisions "one cannot rely merely on
idealistic principles." Particularly when one is making foreign policy decisions it is not sensible to "talk of vague
theoretical things" or waste time on "idealistic" or "moral"
approaches to the situation. Political leaders are every day
working with many forces beyond their control and they
simply cannot always pursue policies that are completely in
accord with their ideals. Thus time and again political
leaders must follow the path of expediency; time and again
they must compromise their principles; and this obviously

puts them on slippery ground. "Opportunism there is un-
happily in every department of human activity," he once
wrote. Thus labor leaders, socialists, and others trying to
make a better world have often been faced with situations
which cause them to betray their ideals. In World War I, for
example, the force of nationalism caused many socialists to
betray their ideal of the international cooperation of the
proletariat of all lands and to support their national states in
the insane slaughter of their fellow workers. Indeed, the
biggest problem facing any politician, according to Nehru, is
that of figuring out how to apply his ideals to the practical
problems confronting him; and it cannot always be done.
Quite often one must choose between evils, and the best the
statesman can then do is choose the lesser evil. This is
especially true in the world of today that is so permeated
with conflict and passion. Thus Nehru has asserted that despite his ideal of a world without colonialism there might be
—in fact there have been—situations in which he would feel
it the lesser evil to side with an imperialist power. Nehru
would very much like to be like Plato's philosopher-king, always able to solve immediate problems in a manner that
would be in harmony with ultimate objectives. But he de-
spairs of the possibility of doing it in a world afflicted with so
many imperfections.[23]

Nehru is aware also that mankind in general and states in
particular are afflicted by what might be called "moral myopia"—an inability to see themselves as they really are, an
incapacity to sense the immorality of their own behavior. It
is quite common, he once noted, for states to praise in good
faith their own acts as morally good and in accord with the
highest ideals while condemning the same acts in others as
immoral and selfish. The British have been particularly afflicted with this weakness, Nehru used to charge in the days
before Indian independence. They repeatedly condemned
Mussolini and Hitler for the same kind of behavior they,

the British, were practicing in India, yet they believed sincerely all the time that their brutality and oppression in India were in accord with the highest virtues and the best interests of humanity. The Machiavellian behavior of states was rarely looked upon as immoral or amoral by the states themselves, and with the rise of nationalism whole populations had developed the habit of glorying in actions which if done by mere individuals would have been considered immoral. Almost all nations, he once observed, have believed themselves at one time or another to be a chosen people, morally and spiritually superior to all other peoples. And the tragedy is that there seems to be no cure for this "moral myopia." Apparently there is an incurable quirk in man's moral fiber. Morally man has failed to conquer himself. His conquest of space is not being accompanied by his conquest of his own nature. Thus in 1956 when the Soviet Union brutally suppressed a rebellion in Hungary, and Britain France, and Israel cruelly attacked Egypt and the area of the Suez Canal, all were guilty in Nehru's view of "grievous transgression of the moral standards freely accepted by the nations of the world." But it did not seem so to the Russian, British, French, and Israeli governing officials. Their behavior, they believed, was morally justifiable and in the best interests of the international community. Given such "moral myopia," the prospects for a better civilization are not bright.[24]

Yet Nehru is quick to add that anyone working for a better world must keep his ideals constantly in sight; he must use his principles as a guide no matter how often he is forced to deviate from them. It was Gandhi, Nehru has stated, who taught him and the Indian people how to apply ethical doctrines to practical politics, and it was from Gandhi he learned that compromise with one's ideals is not the same as deserting them, for the compromise is all right provided it takes one in the right direction, by however devious a route.

It is this approach, Nehru has said, that is one of the reasons for the success of the Communist movement in Russia. Russian Communist leaders have always looked on Marxist theory and ideals only as general guides, diverging from them even to the point of twisting Marxism when necessary. But they have been careful to keep Marxism ever before them as a general guide, being satisfied to apply it to everyday problems as best they could.[25]

The great tragedy to Nehru is that political leaders so often tend, in the rush of practical everyday affairs, to forget their ideals entirely; and to Nehru policies without idealism are not practical. He has no patience with those who argue that policies should be only practical because too often the so-called practical policies of statesmen have led to incessant conflict, misery, and suffering.[26] Much of the strength of the Gandhi movement stemmed, Nehru has declared, from the fact that it was based on idealism and that the actions taken by Gandhi were usually in accord with the movement's ideals. It was this correlation between action and principle that gave the masses a sense of righteousness, a feeling of confidence and power, and made them feel like completely "integrated human beings" whose thoughts and actions were together.[27]

Thus in his reforming drive for a new and better civilization Nehru is as practical as a shoe lace. Like Gandhi, Franklin Roosevelt, and Woodrow Wilson, he likes to picture himself as a "practical idealist" approaching the reshaping of mankind with a pragmatism that makes him see clearly the limitations, as well as the possibilities, of the great endeavor he has taken in hand.

Like most reformers, of course, Nehru has not permitted his awareness of the obstacles to a better world to destroy all his optimism. He is perforce a cautious optimist, but an optimist nevertheless.

This combination of optimism and pessimism was well expressed in a 1933 letter to his daughter. After emphasizing the unpleasantness of history and lamenting that "man, in spite of his great and vaunted progress, is still a very unpleasant and selfish animal," Nehru insisted that he could not help seeing a silver lining of progress through it all. "I am a bit of an optimist," he declared, "and am inclined to take a hopeful view of things." But he was careful, he added, not to let his optimism blind him to the realities and dark spots around him.[28]

The rise and progress of the Soviet Union vastly increased his hope for the future. In a 1936 speech he declared that one of the things about the Soviet experiment that appealed to him was that it not only called for "a new civilization radically different from the present capitalist order" but that what was visible of it in the USSR also gave hope that a new order was possible.[29]

He has never argued that a utopia might be created; "but it is certainly possible," he has asserted, "for us to lessen human want and misery and suffering. . . ."

He admits he cannot rationally justify his optimism. The best he has been able to do is attribute it to his good health, his "sense of adventure and joy in life," and his pleasure in his work. But he insists that he rarely gets pessimistic about the future. "There is in me a sense of confidence in the future," he once declared, "in India's future, in the world's future." Not even the dismal history of mankind has been completely depressing; for the capacity of man to survive, to endure misery and rise again has made a deep impression on Nehru, an impression he has expressed eloquently:

I see in this past the long struggle of Man against adverse surroundings and in the face of innumerable difficulties. I see his repeated martyrdom and crucifixion, but I see also the spirit of Man rising again and again and triumphing over every adversity. . . . History tells us of the struggle of Man for freedom, and in spite of many failures his achievements and successes have been remarkable.

The future appears to be full of conflict and difficulty, but I have little doubt that the spirit of Man, which has survived so much, will triumph again.[30]

Nehru has regretted that so many people have lost their old faith in the inevitability of progress; nor is his own faith as firm as it once was. But the survival and rise of Man after each great crisis or set-back is a wondrous and faith-reviving thing and Nehru is hopeful that if that continues, Man will rise from each future crisis on a higher plane.[31]

Needless to say, neither Nehru nor any other man knows the answer to the world's troubles and Nehru has insisted many times that all he has been able to do is "grope" for workable answers. He has "groped" especially for an answer that might prevent a third world war only to conclude that "I have no general remedy for the world's ills, nor do I feel myself competent to deal with them."[32]

But if Nehru does not know the answer to the world's troubles, there is no doubt that for more than a generation he has had a vision of the general character of the kind of civilization he would like to see, and he has made many suggestions as to how that new civilization might be achieved. It is to this vision—not of a world to come, but of a world he wishes would come—that we now turn.

Chapter II

Rationalism

THE NEW CIVILIZATION and the new system of international relations Jawaharlal Nehru would like to see would have rationalism, or the spirit of scientific inquiry, as a major characteristic. Although Nehru was probably inclined to this view before he met Gandhi, it is in accord with Gandhi's demand that individuals be constant seekers of truth.

For more than a generation Nehru has been in revolt against reliance on authority and faith. It is authority or faith, largely as expressed through religion, he has argued, that has so frequently throughout history enchained the mind of man in superstition, myth, magic, and dogma. The religions of India have been guilty, he wrote in 1926, of having killed originality of thought and of making the Indian people dogmatic and little minded; and "no country or people who are slaves to dogma," he added, can progress. . . ."[1]

But religions, churches, and priests have not been the only culprits. Governments and many other institutions have also been guilty of dogmatizing and of enslaving man by insisting on an irrational and unquestioning obedience to authority and by requiring an unreasoning conformity to an ideology.

Science is much preferable to religion, he has stated repeatedly, for science does not dogmatize. It does not require acceptance on faith or obedience to authority. Instead science calls for doubting, hesitating, rational inquiry. Science also has respect for the human mind and is tolerant of varying opinions.[2]

It was the rationalism and scientism in Marx, Nehru has explained, that attracted him to Marxism, and he was delighted when the Soviets launched their first Five Year Plan and thereby applied the "spirit of science to social affairs." He was not at all pleased, however, when the Russian Communists proceeded to make a dogma out of Marxism; for to Nehru that was a complete perversion of Marx's scientific outlook. And it was this blunder of dogmatizing Marxism that made it folly for other nations to attempt to copy Russia blindly.[3]

One of the most attractive characteristics of Western civilization to Nehru is the rationalism or scientism that has been developing in the West since the latter part of the eighteenth century and which has gone far to displace the unreason, magic, and superstition that had enslaved the Western mind for centuries.

Nehru has been careful to point out, however, that in his appeals for rationalism and scientism he has been calling for far more than the mere application of science. What he really wants, he has insisted, is the scientific approach accepted as a way of life, as a process of thinking regarding problems, as a method of acting and associating with one's fellow man. He wants a civilization composed of men who are adventurous and critical in their thinking, who refuse to accept things without testing and trial, who are willing to change their previous conclusions in the face of new evidence, who are engaged in an everlasting search for new knowledge. Mere agreement without critical thinking is meaningless, he has asserted. Thus young people should analyze critically what they are taught; and they should reject everything "however hallowed it may be by tradition and convention and religious sanction, if your reason tells you that it is wrong or unsuited to the present condition."[4]

Yet Nehru would be the last man to insist that by adopting a scientific approach man could solve all his problems. He is fully aware that there are limitations as to what can be achieved by such an approach and he wants science allied with philosophy.[5]

One of the reasons Nehru prefers democracy to authoritarianism is that democracy is based on rationalism while authoritarianism is based on dogma. Democratic theory demands free discussion and an inquisitive search for truth, he has declared—the very things authoritarianism forbids. Thus democracy brings to political, social, and economic problems an inquiring mental approach. And while democracies are not always as rational as Nehru would like to see them, at least the theory on which they are founded offers a wider opportunity to be rational than does any other state theory.[6]

Rationalism and scientism are also necessary, in Nehru's view, for individual freedom. Freedom has been destroyed in the past, he has declared, in many ways. While India, for example, never had a Pope or a church that attempted to control thought and behavior, the people became enslaved nevertheless by the development of rites, ceremonials, and superstitions that grew up gradually among them. Customs and conventions and the authority of "sacred books" became as oppressive to human liberty as any Pope or church had ever been. But a people dedicated to reason and science could not become so oppressed and individual liberty could flourish among them.[7]

A world based on reason and science is desired by Nehru also because it is through these approaches to problems that the misery of the masses of men is most likely to be relieved. Already, he has argued, science has revolutionized the conditions of human life more than anything else in the long course of history and it is through the continued application of science and the scientific approach that man is being relieved gradually of many of his age-old burdens. Through them the wretchedness of the common people of the earth might be brought to an end and a life of decency—if not abundance—be made available for all.[8]

"Politics led me to economics," he once said, "and this led me inevitably to science and the scientific approach to all our problems and to life itself. It was science alone that could solve these problems of hunger and poverty, of insanitation and literacy, of superstition and deadening custom and tradition, of vast resources running to waste, of a rich country inhabited by starving people."[9]

But Nehru is far too practical to expect the rise of a totally rational world in the immediate future. He knows that despite the progress made toward a civilization based on reason and science, mainly in the West, during the past two hundred years, man still has a long way to go. He is quite aware that a great handicap to the development of a new and more rational civilization is the conservatism or mental lag in man that causes man's thinking to cling to old ways, to lag behind events, and to cherish ancient myths and fancies. Man is essentially a "conservative animal," Nehru has said, who disapproves of anyone attempting to change his ways, and this is a fact with which reformers must reckon. There is a paradox in the mind of man, Nehru has asserted. All progress has been brought about by the intellect, yet the mind lags behind its own creation. He sees this paradox especially evident in the most progressive states where despite the most amazing advances, the people are still hamstrung by a narrow and outmoded nationalism. While in such states there is a new and advancing technology crying out for "one world," the narrow nationalism besetting the population forbids the creation of that world.[10]

Nehru is aware also that thus far man has been an essentially irrational animal, behaving more in accordance with his feelings than with his reason. Man's civilization is only a thin veneer, Nehru holds, that rubs off easily when passions are aroused, often revealing a brutal savage. Savagery was especially visible in the behavior of seemingly highly civilized Englishmen in India who never gloried in brutality as did the Nazis but were capable of it when aroused. The irrational element in man is also visible, Nehru claims, regarding questions of property. Many people, he has declared, attach more importance to property than to their lives and they often get more excited about property than about life and death. So it is no wonder that leaders who appeal to emotions, as most great religious leaders have done, are more likely to be effective than leaders who attempt to make men think. He has expressed dislike of both the unthinking applause and the unthinking condemnation of Communism. And he has concluded that not much of life is logical. Few people are logical, he has said, and those who are extremely logical are likely to get into trouble.[11]

Yet the small degree of progress men have made toward the development of a rational world has not completely discouraged Nehru. He is certain, as were Gandhi, Jefferson, Wilson, and Franklin Roosevelt, that an appeal to the intellect can be successful. It was just such an appeal that the great Hindu revivalist Shankara made with success in India in the eighth century, Nehru has declared. Shankara went all over India arguing with, debating with, and convincing large audiences by reason and logic. Yet Shankara's very rational appeal caught the imagination of the masses and changed the whole mental atmosphere of the country.[12]

There were some irrational people in both India and Pakistan trying to arouse passions and prejudice and set India and Pakistan against one another, he charged in 1953. "But they can ultimately be prevailed upon," he added, to see the error of their ways and to realize that cooperation is better than antagonism.[13]

The progress of science and rationalism during the past

two centuries also gives Nehru a ray of hope. The high degree of rationalism in Gandhi's approach, moreover, was always a wondrous thing to him. Thus he is not without optimism for the future.

The major obstacle to a rational civilization and a rational system of international relations, in Nehru's view, is the great psychological affliction of fear. It is fear, Nehru has claimed, that is the most basic threat to the survival of the modern world.[14]

Fear is everywhere, according to Nehru, permeating and saturating and perverting the behavior of both individuals and nations. The rich fear the poor, nations fear nations, blocs of states fear other blocs, the East fears the West and the West fears the East. The whole atmosphere of the globe is soaked in fear.

And it is this very fear, this psychosis of fear, this climate of fear that clouds men's thinking, that obstructs men's reasoning faculties, that forbids the use of logic and that causes men to do wrong. It is this fear that promotes hatred of one people for another and that time and again has caused men to forget their humanity and that has transformed them into impassioned beasts fighting madly and irrationally for nothing more than survival. It is this fear that causes a decline in intellectual and moral standards and causes people to become neurotic and hysterical and utterly unable to judge anything calmly. It is this fear that distorts values and causes men to revert into barbarism, forgetting all the civilization they have learned.[15]

"This is a terrible thing," Nehru has asserted, "this fear complex that we see all over the world today. . . ." And he has noted more of it in Europe and America than in Asia; for it is in Europe and America that the so-called "have" nations are located and it is the "have" nations that are in dreadful fear of losing their possessions.[16]

It is fear, Nehru has argued, that is the basic cause of revolutions. Many people fear new ideas and the changes that are constantly appearing as the result of the dynamism that is the very law of life. But when those who fear change refuse to accept or adapt themselves to the new conditions, revolution is the result.[17]

It was fear, he continued, that produced the Moslem-Hindu conflict in India that eventually resulted in the separation of Pakistan from India. The Moslems were afraid they would be an oppressed minority in a population predominantly Hindu and it proved impossible to convince many of them that there was no justification for their fear.[18]

There are times when even science is hurt by fear, Nehru has maintained. In 1938 he told a group of Indian scientists that they seemed to have become afflicted by fear—fear that some of their activity might anger the British Government and endanger their security and position; and such an attitude was not conducive to scientific endeavor.[19]

When addressing the United States Congress in 1949 Nehru implied that the questionable unconditional surrender policy of the Allies in World War II was the result of an irrational reaction to fear. He suggested that the overriding objectives of the war—or what should have been its over-riding objectives—of peace and reconciliation had been lost sight of because minds had become swayed and clouded by hatred and fear.[20]

But fear is the cause of greater tragedies than these, in Nehru's view; it is also the cause of more fear. Fear of the armed might of the Communists in Europe after World War II, Nehru has asserted, was the cause of the creation of NATO and the re-arming of Germany, and it was in turn Soviet fear of these developments in the West that caused the

Soviets to organize the Warsaw Pact. It is concern for their
security that has caused the Soviets to hold on to Eastern
Europe, he told a visitor in 1958, and he believed that they
would turn it loose when they no longer felt threatened. He
quoted Khrushchev to the effect that for forty years the Red
regime had had to defend itself from hostility on all sides,
and Nehru thought that if that deep-seated, obsessive, nerve-
wracking fear in the Soviet mind could be dissolved, Soviet
behavior would be transformed. Meanwhile, the United
States was in the grip of the same affliction. The psychological attitude of both nations was wrong, and it was this attitude of fear that had produced and was maintaining the
cold war.[21]

Thus fear creates its own vicious circle, its own atmosphere or climate wherein fear feeds on fear, wherein fear
promotes fear. It was this kind of a situation that was the
cause of World War I. French-German rivalry on the land
and British-German rivalry on the sea promoted a climate of
fear which in turn produced alliances and armaments races
which accentuated the terrible atmosphere, until finally fear
drove all the nations into battle. And it is this same "over-
mastering fear" prevailing in the wake of World War II that
Nehru has repeatedly declared might bring on another war.
He does not seem to believe that the usual type of economic
and political conflict is likely to precipitate anything so horrible as a third world war; but fear by one party of the
increasing strength of the other party might do it.[22]

In thus looking upon the attitude of fear as the most basic
obstacle to the solution of mankind's troubles, Nehru is
really arguing that man's primary difficulty is psychological.
He is arguing that many or perhaps most of the conflicts of society are due to a psychological attitude or at least worsened
by a psychological attitude and that the first step that must
be taken to resolve the conflicts is to change that attitude.

Nehru hastens to add, however, that this obstructive atti-

tude—this psychotic complex of fear—exists primarily because men so much of the time attempt to achieve their goals
by wrong means. They use methods to solve their problems
that literally frighten their fellow men. Then their fellow
men use methods to defend themselves that equally frighten
the original fellow men. Thus a vicious circle is created. The
global climate of fear evident in international relations is
man-made.

The obvious solution to the problem, in Nehru's view, is
that mankind should discard the traditional means used
to settle conflicts—discard the methods that generate fear—
and adopt a set of methods or an approach, as he sometimes
calls it, that will not only not generate fear, but will even
prevent fear or will dissolve whatever fear might accidentally
arise.

Here Nehru is attempting to produce in mankind the
same sort of psychological revolution Gandhi produced in the
Indian masses. Wherever he has traveled he has told the
story of how Gandhi dissipated this complex of fear in the
Indian people, of how Gandhi persuaded the peasants to shed
their fear of the landlord, the money lender, the police; of
how even the well-to-do were persuaded to give up their fear
of losing their possessions; of how everyone was brought to
lose their fear of prison, of being beaten, and even of death.
Then when the psychosis of fear was dissolved, it was possible, so the story goes, for the people to apply new methods,
a completely new approach—the technique of Satyagraha—to
the solution of problems involving conflict. And Nehru implies that all the world would do well to follow the Indian
example.[23]

It is fair to say that the major objective of Indian foreign
policy under Nehru's leadership has been to dissolve the
psychosis of fear that for thousands of years has pervaded the
atmosphere of international relations. As early as 1921, in
the first resolution passed by the Indian National Congress

on foreign policy, Nehru asserted that when given her independence India would have nothing to fear from any neighboring state since no neighbor had any designs on her.[24]
Since getting her independence Nehru has reiterated the
same thought time and again, declaring not only that India
was not afraid of any neighbor, but also that she was not
afraid of any of the great powers despite their huge armies,
fleets and atomic bombs, for India had proved it was possible
to stand before a great power and not submit. India has very
little power of aggression, he has declared. She does not have
and does not want the military strength essential to assert
her power outside her own borders. But her power to resist
an invader is very great. An invader coming into India would
soon discover the entire population arraigned against him,
and he would soon discover that he had allowed himself to
be ensnared in a morass of problems from which no profit for
himself was to be gained.[25]

How apprehensive Nehru has become in the depths of his
heart as a result of the intrusions of the Red Chinese in 1959
through the northern frontier, we do not know. Publicly he
has continued to insist, however, that he does not expect a
general invasion by China. Nor does he seem outwardly to
fear such an invasion even if it does come; for he still seems
satisfied that India's power to resist it will prove equal to the
occasion.

This does not mean that Nehru is urging nations to give
up all their arms and become pacifists, for to Nehru pacifism
has always been a foolish doctrine. He agrees, moreover, that
no statesman can afford to risk the security of his own state;
and every state, therefore, must remain militarily prepared
to resist aggression. Passive resistance is folly. But he does
insist that preparations for war that go to the point of producing fear in others simply bring war nearer. The very
acceptance of military aid from abroad is evidence that a

state is afraid, and if India ever accepts such aid it will be a sign that she too has succumbed to fear.[26]

The most immediate objective in India's global diplomacy is to persuade the states of the world to cease the practice of mutual condemnation and recrimination which Nehru seems to believe is a major generator of the fear complex. It is this diplomacy of condemnation and threat, Nehru holds, that is doing so much to make populations excited and impassioned. Before reason can be applied, therefore, national groups and their leaders must be calmed down; they must be persuaded that their practice of abusing each other, of shouting at each other, of cursing and slandering each other, of always blaming each other, cannot help but inflame their differences and make rational settlements of their disputes impossible to achieve. No matter how wrong a state might be in the position she takes, therefore, calling her names and condemning her should be avoided. Thus India is constantly appealing for an end to mutual abuse and is repeatedly refusing in the United Nations to support resolutions, no matter how justified, that heap condemnation on a nation. He admits that India alone can do little about the matter, but she can at least refrain from adding to the torrent of abuse. Thus in the Korean War she refused to join in branding Red China an aggressor, solely because of the belief that by so doing, negotiations with Red China for a reasonable settlement would be made more difficult.[27]

It is true that by late 1959, Red China's abuse of Tibet and her persistent occupation of territory in the Himalayas claimed by India were on the verge of provoking Nehru to desert these principles and to join the general chorus of condemnation that has characterized international relations in the twentieth century. But what little condemnation he has expressed of the Chinese Reds has been mild. His self-restraint has been almost incredible, as well as unpopular with many of his own countrymen, but there is no reason to believe that he will engage in a general retreat from what he has been preaching.

We shall examine later the precise means Nehru wants applied in international relations in place of the methods now used. Suffice it to say at this point that his theory of international relations has no room in it for surrender to aggression or compromise with evil.[28] But before rational methods of settling disputes in international relations can be applied, before an open-minded or scientific-inquiry type of approach or search for truth can be used, the psychological atmosphere of international relations must be changed; and it is essentially the fear complex gripping virtually all states and peoples that must be dissolved. It is to this end that Nehru has designed his foreign policy.

Chapter III

Tolerance

IN ADDITION to wanting a habit of rational inquiry made universal, Jawaharlal Nehru also wants a general climate of tolerance established throughout the world.

The idea that people should be tolerant of each others' ideas, ideologies, ways of life, religions, and so on is an age old characteristic of Indian culture and was, therefore, normal in Nehru's heritage. It has been noted by outside observers that Indians have always believed that although people in their own societies should conform to their own institutions and systems (i.e., the caste system), no attempt should be made to impose those institutions or systems on others.[1] Nehru too has pointed with pride repeatedly to the religious tolerance that has prevailed historically in India, insisting India was never afflicted with anything like the bitter religious intolerance that blackened the pages of European history and that no religious conflict was known in India until the arrival of the Moslems.[2]

Nehru has never ceased marveling at and praising the rich variety pervading India's culture. He seems to glory in diversity, to exult in differences; and he seems to feel that the best life is a life surrounded by a veritable kaleidoscope of behavior, institutions, systems, ideologies, and practices.

People and their cultures differ, Nehru insists, and it is folly not to recognize that fact. It is equal folly not to respect

31

those differences and give them full play. For differences among people have always existed, he holds, and they are going to continue to exist. Yet much of the world's trouble stems from the refusal or inability of people to tolerate each others' differences, to the fact that people too often become irritated at those who think or act differently. One of the great virtues of the British Commonwealth system, to Nehru, is that it is suffused with tolerance, providing a medium through which the members can cooperate while at the same time each member is allowed to do as she pleases.[3]

A major cause of intolerance, in Nehru's view, is that people too often confuse the superficial differences among people with basic differences. They seem to believe that differences in ways of eating, drinking, and dressing or differences in mental approaches and other cultural characteristics are evidence of fundamental divergencies. To Nehru, of course, all such differences are superficial. He is convinced that most men are similar in their basic characteristics, that they have "more or less the same urges, the same desires;" that every human being, with few exceptions, "wants peace in the world. He wants to get on; he doesn't want trouble; he wants to live his peaceful domestic life. He wants his country to have peace, so that it may progress." Thus there is a great deal of unity underlying all the diversity among human beings; and those who see only the superficial differences, who think other people are entirely different, who feel other-behaving people have no common bonds with them, who feel alien to one another—such people tend to forget that the basic urges and thoughts of all are more or less alike.[4]

Too often these superficial differences among people produce that terrible fear of one people for another that looms so large in Nehru's thinking. Too many people with different ways of life or varied cultures find it impossible to understand one another, and what they do not understand—

the unknown—they fear, and this fear repeatedly produces conflicts.

Even worse, people of different cultures tend to believe that their culture is superior to those that are different and that the cultural group to which they belong is superior to other groups. Most people know too little history to be aware that the superior achievements of any one group are invariably temporary and that virtually all peoples have had both periods of greatness and periods of stagnation.

Thus the contemporary dominance of Western culture provides no justification for Westerners to believe they are inherently superior to the peoples of the East. Asia also has had her great periods, producing all the great religions of the world in addition to magnificent works in philosophy, literature, art, and government. Until the end of the Middle Ages, in fact, European culture was in no position to claim superiority over Asian culture; indeed, for long periods, Nehru has pointed out, Asians were dominant, conquering Europe in wave after wave and long treating Europe as a colony. In ages long gone Asia both ravaged and civilized Europe.[5]

The so-called superiority of the West over the East did not appear, in Nehru's view, until the scientific, technological, and industrial revolutions occurred in the West two or three centuries ago. Through these revolutions the West shed her medievalism and accumulated the military strength that allowed her to expand over and dominate the still medieval East. Nehru does not pretend to know why the spirit of science and free inquiry developed in recent times in the West and not elsewhere; but he does insist that Asian peoples have had similar periods of inquiry and creativeness in the past and that to be temporarily ahead of other peoples as a result of such seemingly "historical accidents" does not justify a people thinking they are superior.[6]

Nehru also seems to have a pragmatic approach to tolerance, for he has argued often that tolerance is essential to a satisfactory world society. A world in which differences among people are not tolerated, he has said, would become "one drab uniform world, a regimented world, with one way of thinking, one way of dressing, one way of eating, one way of doing everything. I don't think it would be a very pleasant world to live in." Thus a pluralistic world society in which there is unending variety is much more interesting and exciting than a "drab" and "regimented" world produced by intolerance.[7]

Who knows, Nehru asks also, which of a multitude of cultures is the "right" culture for a people to have? Although as an agnostic Nehru could not quite go along with Gandhi in the affirmation that "God is truth," he is quite in accord with the Gandhian credo that every man should engage in an unending search for truth. The inquiring, unsatisfied mind that Nehru wants in each man's head is never likely to find "the truth." Quite possibly there is no such thing as "the truth," and what is a truth for one man certainly is not necessarily a truth for every man. In like manner what is the best or true way of life for one people certainly is not the best or true way of life for another people. Each group of people must be allowed the privilege, therefore, of working out a way of life that is "right" for them and their environment.

If you want people to tolerate you and the way of life you believe is "right," Nehru adds, you must also be willing to tolerate them and what they think is right. Although he has never liked dictatorships he insists that he has refrained from criticizing the Communist dictatorships in the USSR and China because: (1) his objections to what they do would allow them to object to what he does; and (2) he does not feel competent to say what is best for the people in those countries. In America also, he has said, there are many things neither he nor India wants, but if Americans want them it is their business and no one else's.[8]

Diversity is a good teacher, Nehru has argued. By tolerating different states and people men learn much from each other, even from those with whom they disagree; and that contributes to the progress of all society.[9]

Tolerance is essential for peace, Nehru insists. If the peoples of the world really wish to avoid war they are going to have to tolerate much that they do not like and refrain from interfering in each others' affairs. Otherwise peace is impossible.[10]

Is not the continuance of a pluralistic, diversified world inevitable throughout the foreseeable future? Nehru thinks it is. Historic traditions are so strong and the lives and philosophies of people change so slowly that conformity among all world society is not possible. And if no power on earth can achieve uniformity of cultures, is not tolerance of inevitable differences the most sensible policy?[11]

It is this principle of tolerance that caused Nehru to oppose an effort in India in the thirties to instill racism into Indian nationalism. By that time the Nazis had made great headway in popularizing the diabolical notion that nationalism was in essence racialism and that if a nationalist movement was to be effective stress must be laid on race and on the idea of hostility to other races. The whole proposal was revolting to Nehru, however; and he was quick to point out that that was not the kind of nationalism that had developed in India and it was not desirable in India.[12]

Wherever Indians have attempted to assert racial superiority or gain special privileges for themselves, Nehru has been against them. He wants Indians abroad to be treated as the equals of all other people. But he has warned them that they will get no help or protection from his government in claiming rights or privileges not granted all people in the states in

which they live. Some Indians in Africa have tried to emu-
late the whites there and acquire special privileges for
themselves, he has charged. But he has reminded them that
they are the guests of the nation in which they are living;
that the interests of the native Africans should come first;
and that Indians not satisfied to accept equal treatment
should pack up and leave.[13]

The proper solution for states containing several races, he
has argued, is for them to develop tolerance for each other
and organize a multi-racial society in which all will cooperate. In East Africa where there are Africans, Indians, Arabs,
and Europeans, for example, this is the only sensible thing
to do. Otherwise there will be constant conflict.[14]

It is this principle of tolerance also that has caused Nehru
to speak out repeatedly against the popular contemporary
habit of many nations to carry on a crusade to promote what
each considers the "right" way of life or the "right" view.
Crusades, he has asserted, are in reality campaigns by one
group of people to impose their way of life on others. Invariably the crusaders are certain that their own objectives
are the "right" objectives for all mankind. But since there
are so often crusades opposing crusades it is self-evident that
one or all the crusaders must be wrong. When, therefore, a
renowned editor proposed to Nehru the idea of promoting a
moral crusade to strengthen the United Nations, Nehru rejected the idea without a second thought. That would be
proselytizing, he told his visitor; and to proselytize was not
characteristic of him, of India, or even of the religions of
India. Today the world is afflicted, he has asserted, with too
many crusades. Many of them are diametrically opposed to
each other (e.g., fascist and communist) and conflict is an
inevitable result. Despite his strong feelings on racialism, he
has no intention of crusading everywhere about it; for that
would merely arouse passions and end up, perhaps, by producing more intolerance than already exists. Thus mankind

would be better off with fewer crusades, with more tolerance, with less desire of one people to impose their will on
others, with more of an attitude of live-and-let-live. And that
is a basic principle of India's foreign policy.[15]

It is also his dedication to the principle of tolerance that
ties Nehru to the traditional doctrine of state recognition
and causes him to oppose basing diplomatic recognition on
such subjective grounds as the supposed morality of a state or
one's likes or dislikes regarding a government. The admission of Red China or any other government into the UN
should be determined, Nehru has argued, purely by the
factual situation. Whether or not a particular government is
morally good or evil is a matter of opinion about which men
differ and the virtues or vices of a government or of a state
should not, therefore, be a consideration. If a government is
actually in control of the territory of a state the fact should
be so recognized. The UN in particular was never designed
to include only like-minded states and admission to its
membership should be open to all states regardless of their
ideologies or types of government.[16]

This insistence on toleration toward all ways of life, all
ideologies, and all forms of government naturally impels
Nehru to favor the principle of self-determination. Every
national group, he has observed, has its own peculiar background, its own historic traditions, and it is unfair for anyone to attempt to impose on them either an ideology or a
form of government that has not developed out of their own
environment and which they themselves do not choose.
When the question of Red China's authority over Tibet
arose in 1950, Nehru declared that "nobody else" but the
people of Tibet should decide the issue. Whether or not
China had suzerainty or sovereignty over Tibet were trivial
legalisms that should be subordinated to the popular will of
the Tibetan people, and he saw no objection to expressing
this view to the Chinese government.[17] When, therefore, a

few years later the Red Chinese government proceeded to
assert complete authority over Tibet without first ascertain-
ing the will of the people, Nehru was sorely distressed; and
he long refrained from condemning the Communist action
only because of his belief that condemnation generates hostility and makes reasonable settlements more difficult.

He is satisfied that an ideology or political system imposed
on a people against their will and that does not grow out of
the cultural environment within the group cannot last. The
Hungarian revolt of 1956 proved, he later told a visitor, that
if Communism is imposed from the outside and if it is contrary to the "basic national spirit" of the victimized people,
it will not be accepted and it will not last. To be successful
it must develop from within as it did in both Russia and
China.[18]

It follows from all this that Nehru is a staunch supporter
of the idea that there should be and can be peaceful co-
existence between the Communist and non-Communist
worlds. He has not always held this view. In the early
thirties he asserted unequivocally that the differences between the USSR and the capitalist states were so fundamental that they could never co-exist in real peace. The best
they could ever hope for was a temporary truce.[19] But by
the fifties Nehru had seen many modifications in both systems. By then also he had seen the cold war between the two
reach a stalemate and he had come to the conclusion that
neither side was strong enough to impose its will on the
other and that in due time that fact would be recognized by
both. It was then that he issued his *panchshila* or five principles of peaceful co-existence: (1) mutual respect for each
others' territory, (2) non-aggression, (3) non-interference
in each others' internal affairs, (4) equality and mutual
benefit, (5) peaceful co-existence. India's whole foreign policy since independence, Nehru stated in 1954, has been
based on this doctrine of co-existence; and while he would be

the last man in the world to launch a crusade for such a principle, he has left an implication that all the world would be better off if his principles were made the basis of all foreign policies.[20]

In 1959 Nehru made it clear again that his faith in the peaceful co-existence of East and West was a firmly held conviction. The rigidity so characteristic of the Soviet Communist approach was not likely to last, he asserted. The inexorable movement of human events prevents anything from remaining rigid for very long in the world. "And, therefore, I have always expected and hoped," he went on, "for progressive reasonableness even in the rigid Communist approach." Communism and Western style democracy would eventually lose their crusading character and learn to live together peacefully just as once crusading and antagonistic religions had learned to live together. Peaceful co-existence was, therefore, well-nigh inevitable.[21]

But despite Nehru's insistence that all nations should be allowed to live as they please without outside interference, he does not carry his logic to absurdity. There are limits to his tolerance. He is aware that occasionally an ideology, a government, or a situation appears that justifies intervention by neighboring states in the international community. A system like that of fascism, for example, based on aggression and violence, need not and should not be tolerated by the community of nations. For any system that becomes a breeding ground for violent aggression beyond its own borders is so obviously a danger to other peoples that intervention is justified. During the years before 1955 when many states were being kept out of the UN by the cold war and there was even some talk of expelling the Communist states and transforming the UN into a non-communist coalition, Nehru considered the whole discussion nonsense. The UN should not be a club of like-minded members, he repeated; and there was no likelihood that all the world would ever become all like-minded. Rather the UN should reflect the world as it is, in all its enormous and exciting variety. Membership should be universal with every state, however, accepting the principle that every other state had the right to live. He opposed the admission of only fascist states like Spain, arguing that they were beyond the pale because their ideologies demanded violence. Aside from such exceptions, however, "the only safe principle to follow is that . . . each country should be allowed to live its own life in its own way."[22]

It would be a mistake to interpret Nehru's repeated appeals for tolerance as the mere mouthing of platitudes by a naive do-gooder. Nehru is far too sophisticated either to mouth platitudes or be a do-gooder in the naive sense of that term. Tolerance is to him nothing less than a super-value—an absolute necessity for the kind of world he is trying to promote. Like all reasonable men of goodwill, he favors promoting international understanding among all the peoples of the earth and he has endorsed the international exchange-of-persons programs and other activities designed to promote such understanding. But he does not expect a great deal to come from them. For he is quite aware that people might thoroughly understand one another, yet remain thoroughly hostile. The animosity between Christians and Moslems in the eleventh and twelfth centuries or between French and German peoples in more recent centuries was not due to misunderstanding, for example. Rather it was due to the refusal of one group to tolerate the existence of the other group or to the determination of one group to dominate and exploit the other.

Nehru is aware also of the fact that asking all men to understand one another and their complex ways of life is asking too much. It is difficult enough for a people to understand their own culture, their own religion, their own ideology; and to ask them to understand also all the other varied cultures, religions, and ideologies in the world is to demand more than mortal man can do. All that is necessary is that men tolerate each other and their varied ways. A tolerant people will not be aggressive, nor will they be afflicted with messianic notions which impel them to impose their way of life on other peoples. A civilization pervaded by tolerance would, by definition, be a warless civilization. Conflict would be blunted automatically by the respect one people would have for the views and aspirations of others, and such conflicts could be handled in a rational, non-violent manner. Indeed tolerance is to be one of the highest virtues in Nehru's new civilization.

Chapter IV

Enlightened
Self-Interest

IN ADDITION to wanting a world that is both rational and tolerant, Nehru wants a world in which the foreign policies of nations will be based on enlightened self-interest.

This means to Nehru that: (1) nationalism is good only when diluted with enough internationalism to allow a considerable degree of international cooperation, and (2) the national interests of a state are prudently conceived only if they are developed in accord with the interests of the international community.

Despite his own unflagging nationalism, Nehru has been an ardent supporter of internationalism throughout the forty years of his public life. It was he, so the story goes, who first made the Indian National Congress broaden its outlook to take an interest in international affairs; and it was also he who persuaded the Congress to realize that the Indian struggle for freedom was actually a part of a global struggle and that it could be made to succeed only if geared into the context of international developments.[1] Nehru himself has given Gandhi the credit for the high degree of internationalism in the Indian movement, arguing that although Gandhi wanted Indian independence, he wanted also a world federation and insisted on thinking of the good of mankind. According to both Gandhi and a leading Nehru biographer, however, the credit for preventing the Indian national movement from becoming narrowly egocentric should go to Nehru. Not even Gandhi had so broad an outlook, the biographer has asserted. Only a few Indian nationalists, moreover, ever got beyond their national horizons in their thinking; and what internationalism they accepted was virtually imposed upon them by the sheer force of the Nehru personality which over three decades pressed them relentlessly in that direction.[2]

Nehru has never had any illusions, however, regarding the excessive power of modern nationalism or the obstacles to modifying it. He has been quite aware that in recent times internationalism was no match for nationalism and that in every contest—in the thirties, for example—nationalism won. He noted that even the USSR had deviated from the internationalism basic to Communist doctrine and had become nationalist, much to the consternation of her friends and sympathizers. Internationalism had been accepted, he noticed, only where it had been in accord with national interests; and this caused him to believe for a time that while individuals and small groups might be able to be internationalists, nations never could. The Indian national movement was exceptional, he thought, for the degree of internationalism instilled into it; but that was all due to Gandhi.[3]

The resurgence of excessive nationalism during World War II seemed to sadden him; but it was not unexpected. Many people had thought that internationalism was on a permanent rise, he pointed out, pushed along by an expanding socialism and by the internationalization of big business through cartels and combines. But whenever a crisis had occurred, he observed, nationalism had reasserted itself and reassumed a position of dominance. One reason for the failure of Communist parties outside Russia in those years, he maintained, was their failure to tie themselves up with nationalism. By insisting on clinging to their tenet of internationalism they had repelled many potential supporters, especially in India, and thus had cut themselves off from the mainspring that moved the masses.[4]

He noted after World War II that despite the lessons the war should have taught regarding the dangers of excessive nationalism, nationalism was still a very powerful force, and in Asia in particular no movement could get far that was not in accord with nationalistic feeling and no counter-movement could make much progress at all. By that time Communists in some places had learned to adjust to nationalism, but nationalism remained a stronger force than Communism. In states where the nationalist movement was leftist or socialist, as in Burma or India, the Communists had so little to offer not already available, Nehru thought, that they were able to make almost no headway.[5]

Yet Nehru is conscious of much more about nationalism than its sheer power. He is conscious also of its very great merits and of the many contributions it has made to the development of modern civilization. It helped build up the nations of Europe, he has asserted, and promoted their great civilization. In recent times nationalism has also been the driving force in the East for freedom and independence. Throughout the world it has had an "abiding appeal to the spirit of man," giving unity and vitality to many peoples. Vigor, growth, unity, and self-esteem are among its magnificent contributions to modern life.

Nationalism is a curse, therefore, only when it becomes narrow and fanatical. Like so many other things available to man—say, religion—it can easily lead man astray. Nationalism can lead people into thinking only of themselves, of their own struggles, of their own misery. It can also cause a nation to become suspicious and fearful of its neighbors, to look upon itself as superior, and to become aggressive. And it is when nationalism impels a state to become expansionist and seek domination over others that it becomes a positive curse and harmful internationally. The French nationalism of the Revolution experienced this kind of evil tendency, Nehru noted. In Turkey also, the defensive nationalism that originally generated a fight for freedom later became aggressive and caused the Turks to crush the Kurds who in the twenties were likewise seeking freedom.

It is always necessary to remember, therefore, that nationalism must remain limited, that it must be liberalized or balanced with internationalism, and that it must never be allowed to develop to the point where the rights of other people are ignored or to the point where hatred, suspicion, and fear of other people develop. When objections were raised in the Indian Parliament to the continued use of the English language as contrary to Indian nationalism, Nehru was quick to answer that while he sympathized with the objections to the use of English to a point, if Indians developed suspicious attitudes toward everything that came from England or America "it will not help anybody."[6]

Nehru seemed to feel that the best way to get nationalism back within reasonable bounds in the colonial areas in which it had become fanatical was to give the people their independence. "Nationalism tends to fade away after political freedom to some extent. . . ," he noted, and it remained strongest where people were still held in the colonial system.[7]

With regard to the relation of national interests to international interests there has never been any doubt in Nehru's mind that the interests of a state do and must come first. He declared in 1947 that:

Whatever policy you may lay down, the art of conducting the affairs of a country lies in finding out what is most advantageous to the country. We may talk about international goodwill and mean what we say. We may talk about peace and freedom and earnestly mean what we say. But in the ultimate analysis, a government functions for the good of the country it governs and no government dare do anything which in the short or long run is manifestly to the disadvantage of that country.

Therefore, whether a country is imperialistic or socialist or communist, its Foreign Minister thinks primarily of the interests of that country.[8]

Here Nehru is stating the most ancient rule of foreign policy—a state's own interests must come first. In 1948 he declared that India's delegates to the United Nations had been instructed to consider first each issue from the point of view of India's interests, and only after that is done should they consider an issue on its merits.[9]

Nehru has applied the rule in daily practice. For example, he has declared that despite his firm belief that no state should interfere in the affairs of another, India would interfere readily in Nepal if need be to protect her northern border. Red China's attempt to extend her authority over Tibet in 1950 did not directly threaten India, in Nehru's view. But he made it clear that if Red China tried to go any further, if she tried to penetrate the ancient frontier of the Himalayas, India would feel her security threatened. Nothing could be allowed to go wrong in the Himalayan kingdom of Nepal, therefore, that might invite Chinese penetration and jeopardize India's security.[10]

The practice of Communists giving their first loyalty to the Soviet Union rather than to their own states has caused Nehru to combat them with vigor in India, to help fight against them all over Southeast Asia, and to condemn the world Communist movement in general. Being a staunch socialist and an adherent to much of the philosophy of Marxism, he has not condemned Communist goals and ideals. Nor has he been willing to be very critical of Communist states. But internal Communists and the world Communist movement that has aided and abetted them and encouraged disloyalty to their own states have often provoked his wrath; they have caused him also at times to have the Indian jails almost as full of Communists as once the British had them full of Indian nationalists.[11]

Despite his oft proclaimed principle in support of nationalist independence movements, Nehru has refused to support and has even condemned such movements when he thought the national interests of India required it.[12] Indian trade policy has also been based on the primacy of the national interest, with trading being done with whatever country it was easier to deal with at the time and with the advantage to India, declared Nehru, being the major consideration.[13]

But this is not necessarily a selfish approach, thinks Nehru; for it is selfish only when a state takes a narrow view of her national interests, only when she thinks of herself alone and fails or refuses to consider the effects of her policy on the other states in the international community. In such a case, a state's policy is not only selfish; it is also foolish; and it might even be fatal. Giving primacy to one's national interests is not selfish, however, if one takes a broad view of those interests, if one considers carefully all the many factors and forces interacting in the international community, if one keeps in mind the interdependence of states and remembers that the welfare of one's own state is intertwined with and dependent on the welfare of the whole community. The trouble with the so-called realists or the so-called Machiavellians is that too often they look upon their state as a thing apart, as a distinctly separate fraction of the society of nations and they fail to see the whole picture. Nehru expressed this view succinctly at the end of a Commonwealth Conference in 1949 by saying at the Conference, "I have naturally looked to the interests of India, for that is my first duty. [But] I have always conceived that duty in terms of the larger good of the world."[14]

The great tragedy of the twentieth century in Nehru's view is that the leading states of the world have taken a narrow rather than a broad view of their national interests; they have not had foreign policies based on enlightened self-interest. The result has been that they have brought misery and destruction to themselves. Surely there has been nothing very enlightened about the way the West has used its great science to bring disaster upon itself, for example. Nor was Japan behaving in a very enlightened way when she copied the West and launched a campaign of imperialist aggression. Japan's true national interests demanded peace and cooperation with China. But by taking a narrow, and therefore a false, view of her interests, she brought devastation upon herself.[15]

According to Nehru, it is doubtful if any great power of modern times has had a worse record than Great Britain in formulating its national interests. Britain's true interests, he claims, demanded that she give up her empire, oppose fascism with all her might, and assume leadership in promoting a new world order based on justice and freedom. But in all these affairs Britain was too slow. Until the very end of World War II, and even after, she followed a policy dedicated to the *status quo,* wishfully thinking that her empire and her practice of exploiting other people could go on forever. The attempt to hang on to her empire was harmful to her own interests, Nehru argued repeatedly. The power of one state to dominate and exploit other people was becoming a thing of the past, for colonial peoples were no longer willing to be exploited and were prepared to fight back. Nothing but endless friction would result from a continuation of imperialism. If, however, Britain should grant independence to her colonies, he predicted, she would find a group of free and friendly nations at her side. By refusing to grant independence she was brewing hostility and trouble which in crises would weaken her. If given her freedom India would go far toward working with Britain, Nehru said in 1939. India would be willing to continue certain trade and commercial privileges Britain then enjoyed in India, and India would accept such financial burdens merely to avoid conflict which would cost far more. India would also be a colleague of Britain in world affairs. "I have loved much that was England, and I should have liked to keep the silken bonds of the spirit between India and England," Nehru explained in 1940. "I wanted India's freedom for India's sake, of course; but I also wanted it for England's sake."[16]

In the mid-fifties Nehru was expressing the same view, declaring that the refusal of the imperialist states to free their dependencies, especially those left in Africa, was contrary to the national interests of the mother countries who would reap from their effort to hang on nothing but "tremendous trouble."[17]

Any state that still based its foreign policy on the traditional conception of power politics was also destined to work against her true national interests, Nehru thought. He had never had any respect for the concept of power politics or for at least that brand of it that relegated morality and justice to secondary considerations. While he agreed that "no nation can base its domestic or foreign policy on mere good will and flights of imagination," he insisted vehemently that a foreign policy in the twentieth century that put mass aspirations, idealism, and morality in the background and had only power as its major objective would be a "supremely foolish" policy.

Thus to Nehru so-called realists like Sir Halford McKinder, the British geopolitician; Nicholas J. Spykman, the American geopolitician; and Walter Lippmann, the American journalist—to say nothing of the German geopoliticians—were not realistic at all. He had nothing but contempt for Spykman's argument that the major objective of foreign policy is power and that such values as justice, fairness, and tolerance should be considered only to the extent they contribute to that power objective. Lippmann's geopolitical conception based on four orbits or alliances was equally objectionable to Nehru. Such a proposal "looks very clever and realistic,"

Nehru declared, "and yet is supremely foolish, for it is based on the old policy of expansion and empire and the balance of power, which inevitably leads to conflict and war."[18]

The traditional effort of states practicing power politics to avoid being encircled while they encircled their rivals did not look like a realistic practice to Nehru. Since the world is round, he argued, every country is encircled by others and however huge a state might be there is always danger of encirclement by rivals. To avoid encirclement there must be alliances and counter-alliances, expansion and conquest. The only final escape is world conquest and the consequent elimination of every possible rival—the very objective Hitler seemed to have in mind.

The only sensible alternative, Nehru argued, was the elimination of the whole atmosphere of rivalry and the substitution of friendly international cooperation to build a new and better world—a new civilization in which states had no reason to fear or encircle each other.[19]

Yet as World War II progressed Nehru saw little reason to believe that the leading powers were becoming enlightened. In all of them he saw a trend toward conservatism, toward hanging on to the old, outmoded civilization that had produced the war, toward a continuation of imperialism and power politics. The war itself had been produced by the refusal of the leading powers to accept change, he asserted. This insistence on the *status quo,* this refusal to satisfy the aspirations of the masses of mankind, had produced the revolt of the fascist aggressors. And while early in the war there had been much lip service paid to such things as the Four Freedoms, the Atlantic Charter, and other ideas envisioning a new civilization, such talk faded into the background as the war progressed. The war's leaders had even ceased attacking fascist philosophy, he declared, and had transformed the war into a purely military affair. A new civilization based on freedom and social justice ceased being a war objective. Yet that was precisely what the masses of mankind were demanding and any foreign policy that did not give top consideration to that objective was not based on a realistic concept of national interests.[20]

With India's independence and Nehru's own elevation to the combined posts of prime minister and foreign minister, he proceeded immediately to apply a foreign policy based on what he considered an enlightened view of India's national interests. India's nationalism was balanced by a powerful dose of internationalism. Realism was combined with idealism. The primacy of the national interests was the rule, but Nehru conceived India's national interests in global terms, in terms that required friendship with all other states, in terms that demanded a maximum of cooperation with other states.

The decision to keep India in the Commonwealth was based on these principles, Nehru has affirmed. Staying in the Commonwealth was to India's interests as well as to the self-interests of the other members who wanted her to remain. The Commonwealth was a cooperative association through which all members profited, and to weaken such an association in a world in which there was too little cooperation would not be to the advantage of either India or the world.[21]

In Nehru's view virtually all the major problems men face today are global problems. Even local problems are now tied up with "dozens and dozens of other questions that agitate the world." While on occasion he has said that certain problems are primarily European and of little concern to India, his usual position has been that there are no such things as purely European, Asian, or American problems— that virtually all problems are global and they are soluble only on a world scale or not at all. That is why the study of the history of individual countries should be modified to allow a study of world history, for it is impossible to understand the history of one country without looking at it in its international context.[22]

The major effect of the Spanish Civil War of the thirties was to increase this conviction in Nehru. The Spanish Civil War was in reality, he concluded, part of a global struggle between fascism and anti-fascism, between militarism and democracy. The fascist attacks on Manchuria, Abyssinia, and Czechoslovakia as well as the problem of Indian independence were all "facets of one and the same world problem." It was not easy for Asian nationalists to see this, he realized; for it was difficult for them to think in terms beyond their own struggle for freedom. But the hard facts of interdependence were forcing Asian nationalists, he thought, to take a broader view; for their independence movements were tangled up with all the other tragic events then occurring in all parts of the world.[23]

India dared not ignore the rise of Fascism and Nazism in Europe, he warned in 1939. The long-sought independence of India would be short-lived if those oppressive ideologies became dominant in the world. Individual liberty and democracy also would become things of the past all over the earth if the dictators of Germany and Italy triumphed. Thus the fate of India was intimately bound up with the fate of all of mankind, and it was her responsibility to take her stand in union with other freedom-loving peoples to avert the deadly peril facing men everywhere.[24]

After the war Nehru reiterated the indivisibility of national freedom, paraphrasing Abraham Lincoln to the effect that the world could not remain half slave and half free, and India's freedom was, therefore, bound up with the freedom of all other colonial peoples. In like manner peace was indivisible, for "the peace of one country cannot be assured unless there is peace elsewhere also." When the Korean War came along he rejected proposals in his Parliament that the Great Powers should get out of Korea, for he was certain that the issues involved in the war were world issues—not merely Asian, as had been suggested—and that to argue they were not the business of the Great Powers was unrealistic.[25]

In like manner Nehru rejected the old idea that the economic gain of one country must inevitably mean the economic loss of another country. Rather he supported the idea that the prosperity of all was interdependent, that a prosperous country was a better customer and a better producer than a poor country. The underdeveloped nations of Africa and Asia, he argued, were a drag on the progress of the whole world and only by helping them rise could all humanity rise. If, therefore, the United States should help India promote her trade, do-goodism would not be involved, for the results would be mutually beneficial. If one part of the world goes down economically, he was fond of saying, other parts go down also. For prosperous nations to help the underdeveloped states to rise was a sheer matter of enlightened self-interest, not generosity.[26]

It was clear, thought Nehru, that there was no real conflict between the basic national interests of states. There were differences in their national interests to be sure, and there were differences in the characteristics of state and national groups. He was aware also that different states gave different priorities to their problems, that what was problem number one for a certain state was *not* problem number one for another state. And this varied scheme of priorities made it hard for states to cooperate smoothly. But to Nehru all these differences were superficial, not fundamental. Thus despite the many differences between India and Pakistan the underlying national interests of the two states did not conflict and it would be to the best interests of both to work cooperatively on their common problems.[27]

All this meant, of course, that the great need in the international system was the coming together of states for some form of cooperation. The national state alone was no longer adequate. It was too small a unit. The smaller states could not even maintain their independence alone, much less promote their welfare to any great degree; and it was doubtful if even the larger states could do so. Ever larger federations and multi-national states such as were represented by the United States and the USSR seemed inevitable and the organization of Europe into such a multi-national federation was one of the goals of the Nazis. But ardent as he was for the self-determination of subject peoples, he opposed the excessive splintering of states; and one of his major arguments against the separation of Pakistan from India was that such a movement was contrary to the trends and needs of the times. The movement for a separate Pakistan was also narrowly rather than broadly nationalistic, he thought, and contrary to the needs of a world that was groping blindly toward federation. The day of separate warring states is over, he declared. "Small states in the world of tomorrow have no future in store and they are sure to be reduced to the status of satellite states. . . ." Partition, therefore, would take the subcontinent in the wrong direction.[28]

As much as Nehru wanted Indian independence, he wanted it within a global federation. In the late twenties he told the Indian National Congress that once India was free he would favor a world federation, even to having India give up part of her "independence to a larger group of which she is an equal member." It must be a world republic, not an empire based on the exploitation of one people by another, he wrote his daughter in the early thirties. "But," he added, "the world is in a bad way and there seems to be no other way to get rid of its illness."[29]

Regional federations or associations including only a limited number of states would not solve the problem, he asserted, and they might even get in the way of the desperately needed global cooperation. It was partly on the grounds that the Commonwealth was only a limited union of states that for several years before independence he opposed India's remaining in it. Such unions, he thought, would simply result in a struggle for power among gigantic associations and the world might be worse off than before. It was on this same ground that he opposed Clarence Streit's proposal for a union of Western democracies, for Streit's proposal excluded too much of the world. Cooperation among states in a region or states with similar ideologies was all to the good, of course; but the basic need was global cooperation, and the idea of One World should be kept paramount.[30]

He was doubtful that governments would have the wisdom to see and act upon this need in the near future. During World War II, in fact, he predicted that in the postwar world another era of imperialism was more likely than an era of international cooperation. The great barrier to the creation of an effective world federation or cooperative system was psychological, he thought, and people's fear of one another would have to be dissolved before anything much could be done. But he seemed reasonably certain that world government, based on the federal principle, would come eventually; and although the world would remain pluralistic and each national state would remain free to fashion its own destiny, all would be subject to the basic law of the global organization.[31]

Throughout all his thinking about international affairs Nehru has insisted that states should maintain a reasonable balance between nationalism and internationalism. He has insisted also that a prudent state will do everything possible to adjust her national interests to the interests of other states —to the interests of the international community.

He knows well that he is here asking statesmen to meet standards that are so high that they are almost unattainable. He is asking the world's people and their leaders to be more rational, more moderate, more farsighted than has been true generally throughout history. He is asking all rulers to approximate Plato's philosopher-king. But he sees nothing wrong with high goals, for he knows that no one knows how high man can go, and the limited successes man has achieved thus far have been due in part at least to constant striving for the unattainable.

Chapter V

Welfare
Statism

THE NEW CIVILIZATION that Nehru would like to see come into being would be characterized also by welfare statism.

Nehru has always been a humanitarian in the sense that he has always been concerned with the promotion of the welfare of the masses of people, who have had, in his view, nothing but a life of misery throughout history.

As year has followed year Nehru has become more and more a *pragmatic* humanitarian. In his own writing he has declared that the better type of mind is one that is governed by "a practical idealism for social betterment." It is a type of mind that is practical and pragmatic, ethical and social, altruistic and humanitarian. "Humanity is its god," he has said, "and social service its religion." Such a mind, he believes, would have ideals that are the result of a synthesis of humanism and the scientific spirit and would represent, as he has put it, a "scientific humanism."[1]

In this description of the "better type of mind" Nehru is describing, of course, his own mind; and what he is really saying is that he is profoundly concerned with the creation of a world in which both the physical and spiritual welfare of men will be much better than it is now and that the scientific approach can and should be applied to promote that welfare.

What he wants economically for India and what he thinks is gradually going to come into being for all the world is a mixed economy. It will be an economy that is predominantly socialist in the sense that socialist principles and ideals will prevail generally, but it will also be an economy in which a fair share of capitalism will remain, albeit a "civilized," "tamed," or socialized capitalism.

The new society would be one with equal opportunities for both individuals and nations to develop with no one part of the world dominating another part, nor with any one nation, class, race, or way of life dominating other nations, classes, races, or ways of life. For no one, he insists, has the right to block the developmental opportunities of others or to impose his own standards on others. Since the thirties, in fact, Nehru has been emphasizing that the equality of socialism has meant to him not so much the equal distribution of wealth (although he wants it to approximate equality) as the equality of opportunity that will give everyone a fair chance to live the good life.[2]

And this good life will be more than a good life economically. It will be also a life in which the values of individualism, democracy, and liberty are respected as highly as they have ever been respected in their great haven, the West; and when fused with the mixed economy of a welfare state, they will be applied more in actual practice than has usually been the case, even in the West.

We have noticed already that as a youth Nehru had a strongly developed sympathy for the underdog and was usually found siding with rebellious forces in every movement designed to overthrow or control the upperdog. By 1927 he appears to have been completely converted to socialism; and in that year he participated enthusiastically in a socialist congress in Brussels, where for the first time he came into direct contact with socialist leaders from other parts of the world. A four-day visit to Moscow the same year rounded out his final conversion; for while he saw much in Russia he did not like, he liked enough of the socialism he saw in actual practice to become completely convinced that socialism was the great necessity for the future promotion of human welfare.

It is worth remembering that in the twenties when Nehru was turning against the capitalistic system he was turning against *laissez-faire* capitalism—the type of capitalism that was still in vogue in most of the world. At that time not even the United States had emerged completely from the control of "robber barons." The reform movement known in American history as the Progressive Era had made no more than a small dent on either monopolies or the nefarious practices of "big business"; and the investigations to be carried on during the Great Depression of the thirties were to show that many of the complaints against the capitalistic system were justified. Nehru and his fellow socialists were not alone in their revolt against it. Thus Nehru was rebelling against capitalism when it was still in its sordid, anti-social, uncivilized state—a stage it is now difficult to remember.

It is worth remembering also that when Nehru saw socialism in operation in Russia in 1927 he was seeing it in what in many respects was its best era. The fearful violence of the Civil War years had given way in 1921 to the era of the New Economic Policy. Much private enterprise had been restored. The collectivization of the peasants had not yet begun. A small semblance of individual liberty—uncommon in almost any period of Russian history—was being permitted. The Stalinist reign of terror was still several years in the future. Great plans for the industrialization of the country were being made and on every hand there were signs of efforts to apply science to the betterment of human life. The experiments being carried on in education, penology, health, and many other fields were wondrous to people from backward countries. So it is not odd that Nehru looked upon much of what he saw as the hope of the future, and the wave of the future. The *laissez-faire* capitalism that then prevailed in most of the world was simply incompetent, he believed, to promote further the well-being of the masses of men, and it was especially unsuited to the East where, like Russia, progress was needed in a hurry.

It was largely in the early thirties when the capitalistic system was floundering almost everywhere that Nehru expressed most of his complaints against the system. By that time he had become well versed in Marxism, had accepted as his own many of the major tenets of Marxism, and viewed the whole capitalistic system through Marxian-tinted glasses. Like Marx, Nehru paid tribute to capitalism for all the good it had produced in the world; for he was quite aware that in spite of the "terrible human misery" that had been a by-product of capitalism in its most uncivilized days, it had promoted knowledge, science, medicine, sanitation, and many other good things.[3]

During those years of global economic depression, however, Nehru was unable to envision the reformation of the capitalistic system so that it might survive and become a better answer to the problem of production and distribution than socialism or even be as good an answer. All he could see then was that capitalism was a dying economic system being driven to oblivion by its internal conflicts and weaknesses. He declared in 1932, for example, that the world was in the "twilight of capitalism, which has lorded it for so long over the world." And he was delighted that it was on the way out; for "when it goes, as go it must," he added, "it will take many an evil thing with it."[4]

The whole system probably would have been done to death by World War I, he thought, had not the United States kept it alive by artificial injections—by loans to Europe that kept international trade moving until the Depression put an end to such stimulants. But what World War I had

failed to do the global Depression was doing and Nehru was
reasonably certain in the early thirties that capitalistic civilization was on its deathbed.[5]

In his writings in the thirties Nehru expressed all the
complaints against capitalism then being voiced by Marxists
who wanted capitalism totally abolished as well as the complaints voiced by anti-Marxist liberals who were campaign-
ing for mere reform of the system. He gave the usual
Marxist explanation of society as being determined by the
mode of production, adding the well-known idea that virtually all societies of recorded history had been class societies
characterized by class struggles and an unequal division of
wealth. The inability of the capitalistic system to achieve a
more equitable distribution of wealth was, indeed, one of
Nehru's chief complaints against capitalism. The industrial
revolution had made it possible, he argued, to solve the
problem of production so that an economy of scarcity no
longer needed to exist. There no longer needed to be any
poverty, hunger, or misery based on a shortage of material
goods. But capitalism had shown no capacity to solve the
problem of distributing the enormous new wealth created.
The problem of food rotting while people starved was a
problem the capitalistic system seemed incapable of resolving.
It was indeed the existence of an abundance of goods and
surpluses on the one hand and scarcity and privation on the
other hand that Nehru saw as one of the fatal contradictions
in capitalism. It was a contradiction that could be tolerated
no longer, moreover, because the masses of mankind had
developed aspirations for higher living standards; and an
economic system incapable of improving the conditions of
the masses—as capitalism then seemed incapable of doing—
had, in Nehru's view, no chance of survival. The only place
in the world in which there was evidence that the problem
was on the way to solution, he declared, was in the Soviet
Union where socialism had replaced capitalism and where

such things as unemployment and inequitable distribution were no longer problems; and this was evidence that socialism might provide the cure.[6]

Nehru condemned capitalism in those days on the ground also that it perpetuated a class system, class conflicts, and the domination of all society by one class—the property-owning, managing, and organizing class. He accepted the Marxian view that all society was "rigged" in favor of this dominant class. Small as it was, this dominant class, rather than the producers, got most of the wealth, he declared. All governments were class governments, he maintained, and all "laws were class laws." Thus it was no wonder that labor unions were legally prohibited for so long. The national economic policies of state after state, particularly those policies described by the phrase "economic nationalism," were designed also largely to benefit the vested interests of the dominant class.[7]

The capitalistic system was also incompatible with the modern urge toward democracy, thought Nehru. Although democracy and capitalism had grown up together in the nineteenth century, there was a basic contradiction between them; for democracy stressed control by the many while capitalism stressed control by the few. Democracy also implied equality, but capitalism ordained a hierarchical class structure and inequality.[8]

Capitalism was also predicated on a human characteristic that had come to be considered immoral in modern thinking, noted Nehru. It was predicated on the "acquisitive instinct," on greed. It demanded that men continue to acquire and hold and acquire again all sorts of things, including profits, sources of raw material, markets, labor, and what not. And, said Nehru, "any system which is based on what is called the acquisitiveness of society is absolutely out of date; in modern thinking it is also considered immoral. Indeed, one of the aims of the kind of socialism Nehru advocated was to limit the acquisitiveness of man.[9]

It was also capitalism, Nehru avouched, that was largely responsible for the excessive development of nationalism in the late nineteenth and early twentieth centuries; and since this over-developed nationalism had produced a revival of imperialism, the capitalistic system was responsible also for modern imperialism. Following somewhat in the path of both Marx and Lenin, Nehru argued that by the latter part of the nineteenth century technological developments had so promoted the interdependence of states that an internationalized economy was the only kind of economy that could serve the needs of mankind properly; but the vested interests that controlled the governments within the various capitalistic national states had rejected categorically the idea of internationalism. Rather they had promoted economic nationalism, especially high tariffs and monopolies; and in their search for ever expanding markets and raw materials they had promoted a new wave of imperialism. In due time, therefore, the industrialized national states had become more intense rivals than ever before, glaring at each other across their national boundaries, promoting hatred of all foreigners, widening the gulf between group and group within the human brotherhood, and eventually fighting colossal wars among themselves. In Nehru's view competition, conflict, and exploitation were inherent characteristics of capitalism; and a system based on characteristics wherein friction was inherent was no longer suitable in an interdependent world in which cooperation was so essential. The very solutions to its problems the capitalistic states were applying, such as self-sufficiency and cartels, actually made matters worse and accentuated national rivalries. Thus the capitalistic system had shown no capacity to adjust to the new era being produced by science. It was high time for capitalism to retire, therefore, in favor of socialism, a system designed to promote international economic cooperation.[10]

It must be emphasized, however, that Nehru charged capitalism with being responsible for only *modern* imperialism—not all imperialism of the past. He was quite aware that imperialism had existed throughout history; and he was aware that it had existed in a variety of forms. In his 1933 letters to his daughter he had described three kinds of imperialism discernible in history. The earliest and most crude form of imperialism, he wrote, had been one in which victors had annexed both the land and the conquered peoples, making slaves of the latter. This had been the form of imperialism the Babylonians had imposed on the Hebrews. A later and more subtle form of imperialism had been the kind in which only the conquered land had been annexed. In this form the people had not been enslaved, for by then it had been discovered that it was easier to exploit them by taxation, trade controls, and other methods such as those used by the British in India before World War I. The third and most subtle kind of imperialism, the one being used by modern capitalism, was a kind in which neither the land nor the people were annexed but wherein only the wealth-producing elements such as markets and raw materials were taken over. This was a nearly perfect type of imperialism since it was so "invisible" that the people were slow to notice it and resentment against the dominating foreigners was slow to develop. In this type of imperialism, moreover, the imperialist state was relieved of the troublesome problem of governing the new territory. This was sheer economic imperialism and it was the kind of imperialism the British had begun to shift toward in India during World War I. It was also the type, Nehru was convinced, by which the United States had so long and so subtly controlled Latin America. The empire of the United States was almost entirely an economic empire, Nehru asserted; for the major imperial interest of the United States had been financial profit and she had been content to control only the economies of other countries. Aside from the Philippines, therefore, she had not annexed much land.[11]

But regardless of the crudity or subtlety of the type of imperialism applied, all forms of it, Nehru insisted, revealed a common characteristic: they all involved the exploitation of one group of people by another. Thus capitalistic imperialism with all its invisibility and subtlety was as evil in its goal as any other form, and there was no place for it in the kind of civilization Nehru hoped to see in the future.

Nehru also charged capitalistic imperialism with being largely responsible for the lack of progress in the so-called backward or underdeveloped areas of the world. India's progress in particular had been stunted by British imperialism, he claimed. Before the arrival of the British, India had been a relatively advanced commercial nation with both economic and cultural contacts with other Asian states. India also had a relatively advanced industry, especially in textiles. But the British had changed all that by isolating India from her neighbors and limiting India's contacts almost exclusively to the British Isles. The British also had destroyed most of India's commerce and industry and had propped up and maintained an already dying system of feudal princedoms. Were it not for this imperialistic interference throughout much of Afro-Asia, many of the peoples of the area would have advanced as Japan had advanced, throwing off feudalism in due course and adopting in due course also the science and technology that had made it possible for the West to move ahead. During the era of capitalistic imperialism, Nehru charged, "Europe has changed out of recognition, Japan has transformed herself with amazing speed, America has become the wealthiest country in the world." But India and other countries under colonial control were prevented from achieving such progress.[12]

There was never any doubt in Nehru's mind, however, that capitalistic imperialism was a fast-dying institution and that within a few years it would be gone because of its utter unsuitability to twentieth-century conditions. After World War II he argued that imperialism had already declined to such an extent that many of the old charges against it were no longer valid, for what little was left of imperialism was quite different from what had existed in the prime days of empire. He even praised England for the graceful manner in which she was bowing out and tackling the problems of her swiftly disintegrating empire.[13]

This did not mean that Nehru's fear of capitalistic imperialism was all gone. The new wave of militarism spawned by World War II and the cold war caused him to fear, momentarily at least, a new era of colonialism based on an urge to control natural resources such as uranium needed by the major powers for military purposes. Nor was he certain that the so-called self-government being granted by imperial powers was in all cases going to be real self-government, since in some places, such as Algeria or South Africa, a European minority long established in the country was being left in control both politically and economically; and it was a minority that was even more reactionary than the dominant groups at home since it had been more or less isolated from the liberal movements of the West. In such a situation, the native majority might remain a long way from self-government and the capitalistic owners of the resources would continue their nefarious exploitation.[14]

By far the most bitter charge Nehru laid against capitalism was that it was responsible for fascism. To him fascism was the ideology to which capitalism and imperialism turned in a desperate, last-ditch stand to save itself. In every country, he argued, the masses were developing aspirations for standards of living that capitalism, then wallowing in economic chaos, seemed unable to satisfy. The masses were demanding

an ever larger share of the goods their labor produced, and
in some places they were complaining loudly. This so frightened the possessing classes that they had become willing to
resort to any method in their desperation to hang onto their
wealth and privileges—including their empires. Rather than
give in to the masses they had renounced democracy, resorted to violence, and adopted fascism as a creed. What
made it worse was the fact that the incapacity of capitalism
to meet the new needs had also produced socialism. "Communism is the outcome of widespread misery due to social
conditions," he wrote in 1933; and in 1950 he was still saying
the same thing. And it was this mass revolt against misery—
in some places appearing as a liberal reform movement, in
other places appearing as a socialist movement—that had
frightened the capitalists still further, driving them into a
fight to the death to preserve the old order against the new.[15]

Fascism appears, Nehru believed in the thirties, "when
class conflicts between an advancing socialism and an en-
trenched capitalism become bitter and critical." Capitalism
could tolerate democracy, he charged, only so long as democratic institutions were useful in maintaining power and
keeping down labor. When no longer useful for that, democratic institutions were scrapped for fascist methods of violence and terror. Nehru virtually sneered at the oft-heard
argument that conservatives are dedicated to the concept
of "law and order." This was merely a disguise used to help
them hang on to their privileges, he asserted; and when
those privileges were threatened the conservatives were the
first to violate law and order as they had done in the Irish
Ulster rebellion of 1912-14. The conservatives favored law
and order only so long as law and order were on their side.[16]

As the years of the thirties went by Nehru seemed to
become more and more bitter against what he insisted was
the tendency of capitalism to adopt the ideology and practices of fascism. It was bad enough, he seemed to think, for

Italy and Germany to go all the way to fascism. But the sight of a hitherto liberal state like Britain going the same way made him both angry and sad. The behavior of the British Government in the Anglo-German Naval Treaty of 1935, in Mussolini's attack on Ethiopia, and in the Spanish Civil War was all in support of fascism, he charged. In her empire the British were leaning more and more toward the use of fascist methods, even to the point of operating concentration camps. And there seemed no way out. The rising tide of socialism had so frightened the possessing classes everywhere that they had resorted to fascism to save themselves, and the struggle had become world-wide. Since the two systems were inherently antagonistic, violence between them seemed inevitable.[17]

In all this, states like England and France were actually working against their own best interests, Nehru believed. National self-interest demanded that England and France protect the Spanish Republican Government because of Gibraltar and Suez. But so desperate had the British and French possessing classes become that they were willing to sacrifice their nations for their class interests. And it was this kind of behavior by Britain and France that was whetting the appetites of Hitler and Mussolini, ruining the League of Nations, allowing Japan to attack China, preventing cooperation with the United States to check aggression, causing the betrayal of states like Czechoslovakia, and in general producing a chaotic and lawless world.[18]

Near the end of World War II Nehru was still expressing the same views, virtually seething with disgust of the British for their earlier appeasement of fascism. It was the pro-fascist tendency in both British foreign policy and her behavior toward her colonies that made it hard for Nehru to support the British when finally in World War II they needed help, he confessed. By then the high correlation between fascism, imperialism, and racialism was more apparent than ever in his mind; and he was still insistent that capitalism—the father or intensifier of these evils—could not be counted upon to produce the kind of world he wanted to see emerge from the global conflict.[19]

Throughout what might be called Nehru's Marxist years he also charged capitalism with being the major cause of modern warfare. Feeling as he did that capitalism could not survive, much less flourish, without the elements of domination and exploitation, he argued logically that imperialism was an inherent characteristic of capitalism; and so long as imperialism lasted, there were bound to be wars among the rival imperial powers as well as between the exploiter and the exploited. Dominated peoples would work perpetually to subvert the existing order. The greed of the imperialist powers—now all industrialized powers—would drive them constantly against each other in their struggle for raw materials and markets. World War I was decidedly a capitalistic imperialists' war, in Nehru's view during the thirties, precipitated by the desire of industrialists to secure opportunities to exploit more areas of the world, of financiers to make more money, and of armaments makers to increase their profits. It was veritably a "rich man's war."[20]

Nehru was aware, of course, that warfare is the result of multiple causes and that in history one can find many different kinds of wars. In one period, for example, wars were essentially religious and dynastic, he pointed out, whereas today they were essentially political and economic. Behind all wars, however, the economic factor had been predominant. In today's wars the economic factor overshadowed everything else, including nationalism. As industrialism had developed, moreover, the economic factor had become more powerful.[21] It was the economic factor, he seemed to believe in the late thirties, that had produced Chamberlain's appeasement policy and was daily bringing closer the war then impending. Had Chamberlain been

more concerned with the true interests of Great Britain and
less concerned with saving British capitalism and imperialism, he would have cooperated with both Russia and the
United States to check fascist aggression and to maintain the
peace. But his fear and hatred of Russian communism and of
American democracy were too great for Chamberlain to bring
himself to cooperate with those states. Chamberlain preferred
economic and political collaboration with fascism, despite
his dislike of the aggressiveness of fascism, for fascism was
supposedly the bulwark of both capitalism and imperialism
against revolutionary communism and a reforming type of
democracy aimed at stripping the possessing classes of their
power. But rivalry between British and German imperial-
isms eventually prevented such collaboration and World War
II had been an inevitable result.[22]

Here indeed was a severe indictment of capitalism, and
an indictment that Nehru continued reiterating until virtually the end of World War II. Nor was it the indictment
of a mere reformer. Rather it was a condemnation by a
revolutionary, by a man who saw little or no hope of reforming capitalism and who insisted that the system as a whole
would have to go; that in due time, in fact, it *would* go,
dragged into oblivion by the weight of its own weaknesses,
by its sheer inability to meet the needs of modern society.

It began to become apparent shortly after the end of
World War II, however, that Nehru's bitter antagonism to
capitalism was being modified. We have noted that throughout the nearly twenty years after 1927 it had been *laissez-
faire* capitalism that he had been condemning; it had been
laissez-faire capitalism the death of which he had been pre-
dicting. But he could not help noticing in the years after
the war that the capitalism that was emerging from that

holocaust was considerably different from the capitalism he had been lambasting. Verily, *laissez-faire* capitalism had died or was on its death-bed everywhere in the world, exactly as he had predicted. Real democracy representing the voices of the masses had risen finally in nation after nation and had pushed through a reformation of the capitalistic system that Nehru had long believed impossible. In the United States, for example, the Roosevelt New Deal had so reformed the nation's economic system that it was unrecognizable from what it had been a generation earlier; and in nation after nation capitalism had been civilized, tamed, toned down, and many of its old evils extirpated by the insistent demand of the masses. The resurgence of real working democracy had stopped the rich from getting richer and the poor from getting poorer. For virtually the first time in history so-called capitalist states were getting the possessors of wealth under control and were working vigorously to provide a better life for the masses. All this was being done, of course, by the injection of a strong dose of socialism into capitalist states. Government control of the economy, largely for the benefit of the masses, was becoming commonplace throughout the earth. Social security programs, public housing programs, public health and education programs, the control of monopolies, graduated income taxes to prevent excessive profits, and many other such schemes designed to abolish mass misery were being developed in even the hitherto most conservative capitalistic nations. In some places some of the major industries and means of transportation were being nationalized. Obviously, the capitalist states were becoming welfare states. And it seemed to be working, for many of those states had become more productive than ever before, and the living standards of the masses had been raised to unprecedented heights. In such capitalistic states many evils remained, but the capitalistic states seemed to have adopted many of the goals and ideals the socialists had been advocating for a hundred years, and this meant that they were moving in the right direction.[23]

Thus Nehru finally came to the conclusion that it was no longer necessary to abolish the capitalistic system as a whole. All that was necessary now was that the reform of it be continued, with stronger and stronger injections of socialism until a new economy combining both capitalism and socialism emerged.

This retreat from his earlier revolutionary socialist position was not pleasing, of course, to many of Nehru's radical followers, and it was especially irritating to Communists. To them he was deserting the faith.

All Nehru had done, however, was to change his views as economic, social, and political conditions changed. His thinking moved on while the thinking of many of his old comrades remained mired in old ruts. He continued to proclaim from the housetops that he was still a socialist. He continued to assert in speech after speech, in written statement after statement, and in the economic plans developed for India that he still believed the socialist approach essential for a successful attack on contemporary problems, especially in the underdeveloped nations. His great sin to his old revolutionary supporters lay, apparently, in his willingness to let some of the new reformed capitalism remain, in his willingness to accept welfare statism or a mixed economy in place of a completely socialized society.

But Nehru was undismayed by the painful cries of those old comrades. He had little patience with people unwilling to change their views as conditions changed, with people unwilling to revise their conclusions when new evidence became available. Those who refused to examine dispassionately the new facts available were not being scientific, he knew; and for a socialist to fail to look at things with the attitude of a scientist was, in his view, the cardinal sin.

Nehru had always been a rather independent thinker about socialism, as he was about everything; and about the Communist brand of socialism he had always been somewhat critical. Throughout all the thousands of words of praise he had heaped on Communism and Communists and the valiant efforts being made to achieve the goals of socialism in Russia there had run the steady refrain that he did not like the Communists' methods. As a follower of, if never a complete convert to, Gandhi's theory of non-violence, he had never been able to accept the view of Marx and Lenin that capitalism must be overthrown in most places by violent revolution. As one gradually converted to Gandhi's theory that only good means can produce good results, he found many other Communist tactics he had never been able to approve. Lenin's idea that a Communist party, to be effective, must be a conspiratorial organization was abhorrent to his liberal attitude requiring all men to act openly. Lenin's thesis that deception, thievery, murder, or any action at all bringing the goal of Communism closer was morally justifiable could find no accommodation in Nehru's moral code.

As one who believed in both individualism and the democratic principle of government by consent, Nehru could see no need for the dictatorship of the proletariat, which implied that the bourgeois minority had no rights; nor did he see any merit in the police state totalitarianism being applied in Russia and supported, apparently, by Communists everywhere. Nehru was repelled also by the dogmatism that had developed in Communism. Obviously, there were some principles of Marxism that were valid. Equally obviously, there were some that were not valid. And it was sheer nonsense to attribute infallibility to Marx or the high priests who followed him. In reality no laws of society had been discovered comparable to the physical law of gravity. And it was totally repugnant to the scientism that Marx claimed for his work, and for the scientific approach that Nehru also wanted men to have, to attribute absolute truth to Marxism. Marx had not composed a holy gospel to be accepted blindly on faith, and those Communists who were insisting that Marxism was infallible truth were to Nehru men of little minds and closed minds.

By the end of World War II Nehru was convinced that many Communists were moving backward rather than forward. "Far from being revolutionary," he charged in 1946, "the Communists are actually conservative." Their transformation of a once scientifically based philosophy into not-to-be-questioned dogma was stagnating them, he seemed to think. In 1952 he told the press that he had read *Das Kapital* and that as of the middle of the twentieth century "Marx is out of date . . . ." In fact, he added, many Communists were in some ways "utterly reactionary."[24]

What Nehru seemed to be saying here was that it was no longer only the methods of Communism that were to be deplored. Some of Marx's economics were also now out of date and no longer provided the right answers to many of the problems of the twentieth century. Marxism had proved "too narrow a creed," he declared in 1956, and many of its economic tenets seemed of little value in resolving the dilemmas of backward nations like India.[25]

Unlike those whose thinking so often freezes into dogma, Nehru kept his eyes on his goals. His goals had always been the relief of the misery of the masses and the abolition of exploitation. And when it became apparent that capitalism still had something to contribute to those goals, he did not hesitate to alter his view accordingly.

Nehru had always believed that Communism arose only as a result of mass misery and exploitation—not as a result of historical imperatives as Marx had argued—and any system or ideology that showed evidence of being able to alleviate those conditions could find some accommodation in his mind. But he insisted also that anyone wishing to oppose Communism could do so effectively only by relieving the misery which had given rise to Communism. The mere attempt to repress the Communist movement was bound to fail. The mere anti-Communist approach of the United States was useless. What the United States needed to do, if she wanted to stop the Communist movement was: (1) relieve peoples of their economic wretchedness, (2) oppose imperialism and its accompanying exploitation at every opportunity, (3) become a champion of racial equality, and (4) go abroad as the supporter of nationalism, convincing each nation that America respects the aspirations of each national group for equality, for a place in the sun, for a voice in world affairs, and that she will do all in her power—by deeds rather than mere words—to help each nation achieve its aspirations.[26]

None of these shifts in Nehru's thinking meant that he had ceased being a socialist. Although he had ceased advocating such radical innovations for India as large-scale state or collective farms, the emphasis he gave in the 1950's to the development of public enterprise as opposed to private enterprise in India's economic plans made it clear that he was still essentially a socialist. But his socialism had become so pragmatic that it was really only an advanced form of welfare statism.

There was developing everywhere, he seemed to think, what he called a "democratic collectivism" wherein there would still be room for private property and the profit motive, but wherein the profit motive would no longer be dominant. Society would no longer be essentially acquisitive. Rather it would be cooperative, and individual self-interest would be subordinated to the common welfare. Capitalist states had already gone so far in this direction, he declared in 1958, that there was no longer as great a gulf between capitalism and socialism as there had been.[27]

But the new welfare statism coming into being would not and could not be the same everywhere. In each nation the environment for it would be different, its degree of development different, its problems different. Each nation should be permitted to find its own path into the new era. It was unwise to insist, for example, that India adopt either American or Soviet economics; for India was different from both and must work out her own welfare statism within the context of such unique factors as her "split personality" that was pressed on one side by an age-old tolerance for all ideas and on the other by narrow forms of behavior such as that of the caste system.

In general he continued to favor the public ownership or control of the major means of production and distribution plus a varied social security program that included minimum wages, maximum hours, unemployment insurance, old age insurance, and so on. But he refused to be dogmatic about what should be done specifically even in India. By the time of India's independence, he had become thoroughly pragmatic, even regarding India, refusing to nationalize industries purely for the sake of nationalization; insisting instead, as Chester Bowles has put it, that there be "private ownership wherever it will work, government ownership where that will work, and the use of cooperatives in other fields."[28]

Socialism is really an approach or a process, Nehru insisted on one occasion, arguing that in its essence it is nothing more nor less than the application of the scientific approach to economic and social life.[29] By this he seems to have meant that socialism to him was essentially the application of the empirical method to the discovery of solutions to problems. It meant an approach to problems with an open, inquiring mind uncluttered by social or religious prejudices or by ideological dogma. It meant that solutions to social, economic, and political problems would be discovered by trial and error, by experimentation, and by reason.

Yet Nehru does not want the new welfare statism to be carried so far that it will destroy values that he and much of the world have long cherished.

He does not want the new civilization that is coming into being to be excessively materialistic, for example. Obviously, he wants abject poverty and misery abolished everywhere; and no man in the Indian national movement was more insistent than he that independence would be worthless unless it was followed by a rise in the standards of living of the masses. Swapping British exploitation for exploitation by an Indian ruling class would be of no value. Nor could there be any stability in the world, he thought, until the majority of the world's people were freed from want, for want was too often the cause of revolutions. But he insisted also that there should be limits to the human desire for material goods, for he was not at all certain that a great deal of material comfort was good for either the character of an individual or of a nation. He had no desire, therefore, to provide every person in India with a motor car, a washing machine, or a refrigerator; and he was unfavorably impressed during his visits to the United States at what he thought was an excessive attachment of the people to their overabundance of worldly goods.[30]

Nor does Nehru want the new welfare statism to be carried to the point where there will be no room for individualism. He is quite aware of the difficulties of maintaining room for individualism in a world requiring centralized controls and mass conformity. But he seems to believe that the problem can be resolved by human reason. "Am I a socialist or an individualist?" he wrote privately about 1939. "Is there a necessary contradiction in the two terms? . . . I suppose I am temperamentally and by training a socialist . . . I hope that socialism does not kill or suppress individuality; indeed I am attracted to it because it will release innumerable individuals from economic and cultural bondage."[31]

A reasonable balance between centralization and freedom, he added in 1949, was the requisite in preserving individuality, and he condemned the excessive centralization of government in the modern world. Where it had been carried too far and the state had become supreme in too many areas of life, unhappiness had been the result. The advancement of humanity had suffered also in such places, for freedom for creative genius was essential to progress.[32]

Individual liberty has always been one of Nehru's major interests, and one of his major complaints against the old *laissez-faire* type of capitalism had been that it had not really provided much individual liberty for the masses. In the early thirties he expressed the oft-heard liberal complaint that religious, political, and all other types of freedom were dependent on economic freedom—and a starving, unemployed man was not free. Thus a fight for economic freedom was going on all over the world.[33] Nehru was very insistent also that there was a high correlation between freedom and the progress of a society. Science, for example, needed an environment of freedom for the scientist in order to grow; and in all walks of life, both individual and national development became stunted when the creative activities and abilities of people were suppressed.[34]

Freedom of expression was essential also for the orderly progress of a nation, he argued. In the handling of problems about which people differed, a free exchange of ideas was the only civilized way of developing policies. The suppression of ideas was foolish. What is good and what is evil, moreover, is often a debatable matter and governments have not been known for any special competence at deciding such questions.[35]

Nehru's welfare statism calls for a maximum of democ-

racy, or rule that is, by consent of the bulk of the people.
It must be a consent given, moreover, only after rational
consideration.

Nehru is aware of the vulnerability of democracy to mass
hysteria, to demagoguery, and to self-delusion. The democracy of the old *laissez-faire* capitalism was, for example,
only a pseudo-democracy since it lacked economic democracy, and the mere possession of the ballot without possession also of economic power, did not produce decision-mak-
ing by the masses. In the thirties when Nehru was lambasting the old capitalism he asserted time and again that political democracy without economic democracy was a "shadow
with no substance."[36]

Nor did Nehru think much of the "uncontrolled" type of
democracy he thought had emerged in the midst of the
industrial revolution of the twentieth century wherein the
people were neither encouraged nor given the opportunity
to think. Too often in elections there was more din and
noise than rational consideration and the result was often
the election of "a dictator or a dumb politician" who was
insensitive.[37]

The vulnerability of democracy to error and hysteria was
obvious to him also. The "democratic crowd" is not always
right, he once argued, for it occasionally succumbs to momen-
tary passion. The violence attending the partition of India
and Pakistan showed, he declared, that "even democracy
can go mad; democracy can be incited to do wrong."[38]

But Nehru never let these well-known weaknesses of democracy shake his faith in the belief that when compared
to its alternatives, democracy is far preferable. Although he
was often irritated by the behavior of the masses, he insisted
that his many years of experience with them had given him
a large measure of confidence in their capacity to govern
themselves in the long run. Democracy, moreover, offered
"society something of the highest human values." It offered

equality of opportunity to every individual and the freedom, therefore, of every individual to grow and to make the
best of his capacities. Democracy also implied tolerance, he
thought, being among all forms of government virtually the
only one that was not dogmatic. The democratic society
never said that it had found the right way and the only way.
Rather it boasted of its fallibility, and it maintained always,
therefore, that dynamic and inquisitive search for the truth
that was so important in Nehru's scheme of things. Democracy was, in other words, a mental approach to political and
economic problems, just as socialism was an approach.[39]

The greater efficiency and speed claimed for authoritarianism over the slowness and inefficiency of democracy had
been greatly exaggerated, Nehru insisted. He agreed that the
democratic process often required more time than the authoritarian process, but not much more. In fact, he once predicted that what the Soviet Union had achieved within forty
years with her authoritarian methods India could do in
thirty years with democratic methods. But the methods used
were all-important, for only good means, it must be remembered, would produce good results; and if sometimes the
methods of democracy were slow, it was simply the price
that must be paid for maintaining the great values inherent
in democracy. In the current contest between authoritarian
and democratic systems, moreover, symbolized by India and
Red China, the winner would be the system that paid the
"highest dividends" not merely in material things, but in
cultural and spiritual matters as well. Thus the intellectual
freedom inherent in democracy would be a paramount consideration in determining the final victory.[40]

Nehru never ceased insisting, however, that freedom and
democracy require a high degree of responsibility and self-
discipline. The requirement of self-discipline runs like a
red thread through Indian religious and philosophical teachings; and it is fair to say that after Gandhi took over the

Indian national movement, the entire movement became a training course in self-discipline. For forty years Nehru has been scolding the Indian people like an angry father not only for their occasional outbreaks of violence but even for their pushing and shoving to see him and hear him speak. Time and again he has proclaimed that democracy does not imply loud and persistent shouting. Rather it implies, indeed it demands, high standards of behavior, and an almost incredible tolerance, and self-restraint of an almost super-human caliber. And he seems to feel that it is the responsibility of leaders in a democratic society to promote these virtues constantly.

In Nehru's welfare statism there is no room for violence, no room for the use of force in the effort to achieve economic and social objectives. "We have achieved many things by peaceful means," Nehru has said, "and there is no reason why we should suddenly abandon that method and take to violence." The use of conflict, violence, and force to attain ideals, he has warned, will provoke conflict, violence, and force, and make objectives more difficult to achieve. Then the campaign to make a better life will degenerate into a fruitless war in which the nation's energies will be undermined and dissipated. The violence and force that accompanied the Russian movement to collectivize agriculture in the early thirties is, therefore, utterly forbidden in Nehru's land reform movement. The Gandhian doctrine of means and ends must be obeyed.[41]

Nehru's welfare statism is very insistent on the virtue of self-reliance. He appears to have no patience with the argument that a socialism or welfare statism that renders many services to a people will undermine their self-reliance, for those services are to be the result of the cooperative endeavor of all, not gifts by an energetic few to a passive many.

But in Nehru's scheme of things self-reliance is just as important for a nation as it is for an individual. Each nation should pull itself up by its own bootstraps. Each people should be taught to believe that the building up of their country is their own responsibility, and that any foreign aid that weakens that attitude is undesirable. One of his major arguments against foreign aid is that it carries with it the great danger that people will come to depend upon it too much and that their self-reliance and incentive to help themselves will be reduced. Foreign aid is acceptable provided it stimulates a people to greater effort in their own behalf and does not make them dependent on the donor, and India could use wisely, he intimated in 1959, aid in larger amounts to generate the new economy of which he has dreamed. But he has continued to insist that any aid that makes a nation less able to stand independently on its own feet ought to be avoided as if it were a plague.[42]

Obviously, there is no room for imperialism in Nehru's welfare statism, and this is the basis for his second major objection to foreign aid. From antiquity on, he has asserted, the acceptance of foreign aid has been a risky thing, involving the danger that the donor will end up holding the aided state in thralldom. A state near China once asked for and received military aid, he wrote his daughter in 1932; she got it, but China refused to leave; and after remaining for several hundred years she finally swallowed the aided state into her empire. Foreign aid programs since World War II have been far too political to suit him. Aid used to win allies or to achieve other political objectives is an evil thing in his view and he has repeatedly warned the Afro-Asian nations against it, for obsessed as he and most Asians are with fears of a return of colonial control in disguise, he cannot help suspecting the aid-granting powers of being motivated by a desire to assert or reassert some form of domination and exploitation over the nations they help. He much prefers the nineteenth-century system of private investments which were made by Europeans in North and South America with no

political motivation or political strings attached and which
worked to the economic advantage of all parties. International, non-political aid granted through bodies like the
United Nations is preferable also to aid from particular
states. Aid from particular states is acceptable only if it is
free of anything that might lead to the domination and exploitation of the recipient.[43]

All this suggests that in Nehru's view there is no longer
any great conflict going on between capitalism and socialism.
The old clash between those economic systems has finally
been resolved to a great degree at least by the rise of a
"middle way"—by the rise of a "mixed economy" containing elements of both capitalism and socialism. In due time,
he seems to think, this mixed economy will hold sway
throughout the world. Different nations will proceed toward
it in different ways, and the way each one wishes to proceed
should be tolerated by all the others. In different nations,
moreover, there will be differences in the nature of the
"mixed economy" adopted because of different cultural environments. But the over-all scheme of a "mixed economy"
or welfare statism designed to serve the needs and aspirations
of the masses and to approach, if not reach, a classless society
is likely to prevail almost everywhere eventually.

The major remaining schism of the mid-twentieth century
is over methods. It is a clash between the democratic process
and the authoritarian process. It is a clash between a modified liberalism that insists on a large degree of individualism
and a totalitarianism which insists that the individual must
be almost completely subordinated to the group. It is a
clash also between those who have confidence in the ability
of the masses to make the final decisions as to what should
be done and those who do not have such confidence in the
masses.

In the old clash between capitalism and socialism Nehru
was on the side of socialism. But now that that old feud is

being liquidated by the rise of a mixed economy Nehru is
content. There are still some battles to be fought, but the
great war itself is over. In the remaining conflict between
liberal democracy and totalitarian authoritarianism Nehru
has always been on the side of liberal democracy, and there
he is determined to stay.

This war of methods will be resolved, he thinks, by one
set of methods proving its superiority over the other. The
authoritarian system has a slight advantage in being able to
produce material results a bit faster than can be done by the
democratic process, although that advantage is not very great.
The democratic system has an advantage, however, in that in
addition to producing material results, it maintains or produces individual liberty also.

He has not attempted to predict which set of methods
will win, but he has entered the war with all his mind and
heart, being in the mid-twentieth century one of the greatest
champions alive of the liberal democratic process.

But it is a war, he insists, that cannot be won with words.
It will not be resolved by resolutions, denunciations, or proc-
lamations. It can be won only with deeds. The Western
strategy which has so often looked to him like a negative
strategy of merely being against Communism is, therefore,
worthless. The only effective strategy for the democracies is
to be affirmative—to prove by deeds what good things can be
accomplished by the democratic process. They must prove
by deeds that the human values of a free society can be pre-
served at the same time that living standards are raised, and
they must do it with speed. Sheer railing against Communism does more harm than good and he refuses to engage in it.
But Communism and its authoritarianism can be checked
and the democratic process made a living reality throughout
much if not all the earth if and only if democracy proves
competent to rescue quickly the masses of mankind from
the morass of misery in which most of them have always
lived.[44]

Chapter VI

Methodology

BY FAR THE MOST INTERESTING aspect of Nehru's theory of international relations is that part concerned with the methods states ought to use to manage their relations with each other. In general, Nehru would like to see all the nations of the world apply the philosophy and techniques developed by Gandhi in what Gandhi referred to as Satyagraha.[1] Only a part of Gandhi's thought and only a few of his techniques are applicable to international relations. There is no doubt, however, that it is Gandhi's general methodology that Nehru has tried to apply to India's foreign policy and that he has also tried to persuade all the other nations of the world to adopt.

Probably the most fundamental aspect of Gandhian thought that Nehru has applied to his own foreign policy and has tried to persuade other nations to apply is the Gandhian theory of means and ends. According to this theory the means to an end are equally as important as, and more often more important than, the end itself. Throughout his teachings Gandhi insisted that unless great attention is paid to the proper methods of attaining one's goal, the goal might not be reached; or even if it is reached, the goal will be found worthless if the methods used have created additional problems. The means to an end, therefore, must be the kind that will resolve conflicts, not arouse them. They must be means that in the end will produce a solution that

is to the advantage of all parties. They must be means
whereby all parties will win; none will lose.

As Nehru has translated it, "every action has naturally,
a result. Every right action must have, to that extent, a
right result . . . somewhere, every wrong action must
have a wrong result." It is all as simple, Nehru has added,
as choosing the right road to go some place, for if you do
not choose the right road you might not get to your desti-
nation. In like manner, if a war is fought by the wrong
means, as were the last two world wars, none of the parties
is likely to achieve the objectives for which it went to war.[2]

A corollary of this thesis is that the moral and psychological nature of the means determines the moral and psychological nature of the ends achieved. Thus evil means produce
only evil results. Hate produces hate; violence produces
more violence; ill-will evokes ill-will; dishonesty promotes
dishonesty; and so on. In like manner "only out of goodwill
will you get goodwill"; a friendly approach will eventually
evoke a friendly response; only peaceful methods will produce peace. Thus if a state approaches another state "in a
friendly way, with goodwill and generosity, you would be
paid back in the same coin" and probably in larger measure.[3]

The Gandhian idea of truth also looms large in Nehru's
theory of international relations. Gandhi taught that all
men should be engaged continuously in a search for absolute
truth; and although absolute truth will never be found, it
should be pursued relentlessly. What the truth is must be
determined by each individual. But individuals differ; and
it is essential, therefore, for everyone to feel that his opponent might be closer to the truth than he is; that his opponent's views might be right and his wrong. In every pursuit
of the truth, therefore, every party must be completely honest
and frank. No lying and no secrets must be allowed under
any circumstances. Otherwise the pursuit of the truth will be
made more difficult.

In Gandhism the concept of truth is tied intimately to the concept of God. But in Nehru, the agnostic, it is sheer rationalism. He is equally insistent, however, that the spirit of inquiry should pervade all society and that the search for truth, or for the best or right answer to problems, must be a never-ending process. No one should ever feel certain, therefore, that he has found the truth and that his answers are beyond question. The major vice of many advocates of religions or ideologies, in Nehru's view, is their belief that their own religion or ideology contains absolute truths which should not be questioned. The only acceptable dogma to Nehru is that there is no absolute truth and every man's and every nation's views are entitled to a fair hearing.

This means that while one should pursue absolute truth, the only truth available to mortal man is relative. Every man and every state should hold on to his conception of the truth, even to the point of death if necessary. But every man and every nation should also be open at all times to persuasion to change his or its views, to be persuaded that the opponent's view is nearer the truth, or that both parties are partially or totally wrong and that the truth is quite different from what both parties believed it to be at the beginning.

When applied to a particular dispute in international relations—say the dispute over the status of Berlin—the parties concerned should first of all each be certain in their own minds and hearts that their answer to the problem is the true answer—the answer that will be to the best interest of all concerned, including the entire international community. It should not be an answer in which some of the parties will gain and others will lose. It must be a solution whereby all parties will gain, in the long run even if not in the short run.

The next step is for each party to attempt to convince all the other parties that its solution is the true one.

This brings us to another Gandhian idea—the idea of non-violence, which Nehru has never accepted to the degree advo-

cated by Gandhi but which Nehru nevertheless believes can
and should be applied to most situations in international
relations. The idea requires that everything that is done to
win an opponent to a point of view must avoid harm, and
since violence invariably causes harm, it must be eschewed
at all costs. To Gandhi non-violence forbade not only hatred
but even evil thoughts, ill-will, resentment, and undue haste.
The goal must be to persuade one's opponent that your solution is to his advantage. Thus the Indian independence
movement had to be carried on in a manner that would not
leave any residue of ill-will between the British and the
Indians and in a manner in which the British could eventually be brought to agree that India's independence would
be in the best interests of Britain as well as the best interests
of India and the world. Causing an opponent to lose face
or suffer embarrassment is forbidden, for that is likely to
leave a residue of resentment and perhaps a desire for re-
venge that will be the source of later trouble, and if that
happens the dispute has not been settled completely and
finally.

Nehru emphasized this point in 1953 when he declared
that the objective of both India and Pakistan in finding a
way out of their conflicts should be "to deter causing injury
to the feelings of the other side and to create amicable
conditions, promote goodwill and discourage ill-will." When
discussing at the same time the India-Pakistan dispute con-
cerning water he asserted that the settlement must be satisfactory to both; that it must satisfy the needs of both; that
neither side could be expected to accept a solution that
would interfere with its development program.[4]

He learned from Gandhi, Nehru has stated, always to
leave the door open during conflicts, always to maintain
channels of communication or connecting links among the
conflicting parties. He learned that he must stick to his
principles, to what he believed to be the truth, but always

nevertheless to remain friendly to and ready to talk with
an opponent; for one should always be trying to think one's
way out of a conflict, always willing to compromise on details, and even be persuaded to change one's principles when
shown one's own are wrong. It was especially Gandhi's
friendly approach to his opponents that struck Nehru.
Gandhi literally undermined his opposition, Nehru has emphasized, by being friendly—by his psychological approach—
and repeatedly his opponent's hostility and aggressiveness
"just faded away." It was to create this friendly psychological atmosphere in which reason would replace hostility
and emotion that Gandhi put an end to strong language
and condemnation of opponents in the Indian movement.
At first this caused Gandhi to be considered a weak man,
but it was soon noticed that it was the loud talkers who
were weak and that Gandhi with his quiet and friendly
approach was a man of steel who could be moved by rational
argument but could not be budged by any amount of
pressure.[5]

Nehru appears to be attempting to apply some of Gandhi's
fundamental rules to international relations. In her *Conquest
of Violence,* Joan V. Bondurant lists nine fundamental rules
governing Gandhi's Satyagraha campaigns. Nehru seems to
be trying to adapt five of them to foreign affairs. In Dr.
Bondurant's words they are:

(1) *Self-reliance at all times.* Outside aid may, in the proper
circumstances, be accepted, but should never be counted upon.

(2) *Reduction of demands to a minimum consistent with
truth.* Continuing reassessment of the situation and the objectives with a view to possible adjustment of demands is essential.

(3) *Persistent search for avenues of cooperation with the adversary on honorable terms.* Every effort should be made to win
over the opponent by helping him (where this is consistent with
the satyagraha's objectives), thereby demonstrating sincerity to
achieve an agreement with rather than a triumph over, the
adversary.

(4) *Refusal to surrender essentials in negotiations.* Satyagraha excludes all compromise which affects basic principles or essential portions of valid objectives. Care must be exercised not to engage in bargaining or barter. [It should be added, however, that there is no objection to compromising on details.]

(5) *Insistence upon full agreement on fundamentals before accepting a settlement.*

With regard to Gandhi's nine-point code of discipline laid down for his followers in 1930 and described by Dr. Bondurant, only two points appear applicable to Nehru's thinking regarding international relations. They are:

(1) *Harbor no anger but suffer the anger of the opponent.*
(2) *Refrain from insults and swearing.*

The fact that most impressed Nehru about the Gandhi technique of resolving conflict was that he saw it work, and he saw it work not only in the major movement for Indian independence but in hundreds of smaller disputes between conflicting-interest groups such as labor and management, within India. No man was ever more skeptical of Gandhi's techniques than Nehru when Gandhi first began operating on the Indian scene. But when he saw Gandhi achieve results in a movement that hitherto had been ineffective with the old and customary techniques, and results that created no additional problems, he became a convert.

In time he began speculating on the possibility of applying the technique to international relations, and by the late thirties he was speaking against those who sneered at the idea of "non-violence ever coming into its own and directing the affairs of men and nations." He agreed that human nature was frail and that selfishness, narrow-mindedness, anger, hate, and violence were universally prevalent. But Gandhi's ideas were working in India, he stressed, and they were catching the imagination of the masses. He still did not know how applicable the technique might be to international relations, but he was convinced it was a powerful and dy-

namic thing, that it had sanctions behind it, and if the world
was to progress, something like it would have to replace violence as a means of settling international problems. He
agreed that any system of collective security must be backed
by sanctions, and perhaps there were times when military
sanctions would be necessary. But too often the use of military sanctions provided only a remedy that was as bad as the
disease. Economic sanctions were less effective immediately,
but they were powerful, far reaching, and less risky of
harm to all parties; and it was possible, he thought, to re-
strain aggression by them.[6] Here, indeed, Nehru was groping
his way toward the application of the Satyagraha methodology to the whole world.

By the time Nehru took the helm of Indian foreign policy
after World War II he no longer seemed to doubt the possibility of applying the Gandhian teachings to the affairs of
nations. He was aware, he said, that the Indian struggle
with Great Britain had been unique in history in that it had
been followed by friendly relations. But it had proved, he
added, that physical force is not necessary as an arbiter of
man's destiny; and it had proved further that the methods
used to attain a goal are of paramount importance. When
later on France restored Pondicherry to India after peaceful
negotiation Nehru pointed to the agreement as an example
of "friendly solutions by negotiated settlement" and proclaimed it as a "triumph" for international goodwill.[7]

The Gandhian technique had proved also, Nehru insisted,
that politics can be kept ethical and idealistic; that, in fact,
moral forces such as justice cannot be ignored in politics
without peril. He realized that political leaders must face
realities and they are limited in what they can do by the
receptivity of others to their ideals and goals. He was aware
also that even the Indian followers of Gandhi had never
been able to do more than apply the master's teachings im-
perfectly and in a weak and halting way, with many errors

and relapses. But there was no longer any doubt in Nehru's mind that ideals, ethics, and practical politics could be combined in workable fashion, and he insisted that in his foreign policy he had tried constantly to combine idealism with the national interest.[8]

Thus Nehru has accepted the basic principles of the Gandhian technique as universally applicable to the solution of problems involving conflict. He has continued to apply them to at least some degree, he has explained, in bringing about reforms within India since he became prime minister. A combination of a friendly, cooperative approach and pressure was used, for example, to get rid of the feudalistic system of Indian princedoms, and a similar approach is being used to achieve land reforms.[9]

But Nehru has always been far more willing than Gandhi to use physical force. The situations under which Gandhi would countenance physical violence were almost non-existent. But Nehru has stated repeatedly for more than a generation his belief that there are situations in which physical violence is both necessary and justifiable. This defense of violence that appeared in Nehru's speeches after his 1927 visit to Europe disturbed Gandhi. But Gandhi's worry did not change Nehru's views. In the early thirties Nehru asserted that "non-violence is no infallible creed with me, and although I greatly prefer it to violence, I prefer freedom with violence to subjection with non-violence."[10]   He did not hesitate to use military force to take over Hyderabad in 1948.

Nehru has been especially insistent that when a state is invaded physical resistance is both necessary and justifiable. In his view the Czechs should have resisted Hitler militarily in 1938. He differed from Gandhi in World War II also in asserting that if India were invaded by the Japanese, India should cooperate militarily with the British to resist rather than offer only the non-violent cooperation to the British that Gandhi preferred. The United Nations was justified also, he held, in checking the North Korean military invasion of South Korea. India, moreover, maintains military forces, with every intention of using them against any invader from the outside, be it Pakistan in Kashmir, Red China in the Himalayan border states of Nepal, Sikkim, and Bhutan, or against any other states that apply armed aggression against India or her nearly strategic frontiers. Indeed, pacifism is a foolish, negative doctrine to Nehru. Pacifists are too often unconscious tools of reaction and sometimes they are even tools of warmongers. Pacifists actually encourage aggression, in his view; and their doctrine of non-violence is a far cry from the dynamic, powerful, aggressive Gandhian doctrine of non-violence that mobilizes great power and uses it in a creative fashion. Pacifists will surrender themselves to evil and violence, he has declared, but the Indian doctrine is against political and moral surrender to evil. As Nehru sees it, there are numerous situations in which even the Indian doctrine will not work and violence becomes necessary. Thus it is asking too much to ask states to give up all their defense forces. They must be prepared to defend themselves in the event things go wrong. In pushing peace programs it is not necessary to give up all military precautions. All he asks is that violence and the military method should not be emphasized, that it be subordinated and that it be looked upon as a technique to be used only in the most exceptional situations.[11]

In Nehru's view the most immediate need in international relations is the transformation of the psychological atmosphere from one permeated by hostility, suspicion, and fear to one permeated by calm rationalism, tolerance, friendliness, and cooperation. For it is precisely such a new atmosphere, a new climate of opinion, that is a prerequisite to

agreement on the various issues and conflicts that exist and
that will continue to rise until the end of time. Conflicts
will be with us forever more. It is a law of life that men
shall differ. But given the right climate of opinion, solutions
acceptable to all parties can be found in time—and without
violence. While he agreed, therefore, that the United Nations
was justified and had even the compelling duty to repel the
North Korean invaders by force, once that was done the
great need to settle the festering dispute was an atmosphere
devoid of threats, suspicions, and fears; and that is what
India vainly tried to inject into the situation. It is such a
new atmosphere, he has said repeatedly, that is also a
prerequisite for the settlement of his own dispute with Pakistan. It is such a new climate of opinion, moreover, that is
prerequisite for the ending of the cold war. And it is such a
new atmosphere that will be essential throughout the future
to protect all humanity from war and aggression, especially
now that even small powers have the possibility of getting
nuclear weapons in their grasp and can cause no end of
mischief unless there is a universal insistence among mankind that peace, cooperation, and friendliness must prevail.[12]

The "working formula" of Indian foreign policy has been,
therefore, to do nothing that will contribute to the international atmosphere of hostility, but to do everything possible that will transform that atmosphere into one conducive
to the tackling of disputes in a civilized manner.[13]

Nehru's chief complaint against most of the nations of
the world is that they persist in using methods to settle
their disputes that augment the climate of hostility rather
than reduce it. Instead of approaching the USSR with a
desire for friendship after the revolution of 1917, for example, the West refused recognition, attempting to isolate
her and treat her as a pariah. The result was that the West
turned the new Soviet state into a bitter opponent. Having
learned nothing from that, the West proceeded to treat Red

China in the same fashion, again reaping the same bitter-
ness and causing the whole world to suffer.[14]

The approach of the Communists to their foes has been
equally foolish, both inside and outside their own countries,
Nehru has asserted. Although he has been an ardent admirer
of the goals, ideals, and achievements of the Communist
movement since 1917, he has been repelled repeatedly by
both their dogmatism and their methods, holding that their
continued use of threats, coercion, and violence cannot possibly succeed in bringing about the new kind of civilization
to which they aspire.[15]

The diplomatic methodology used by the United States
and the Soviet Union in the cold war is, in Nehru's view,
nothing less than a perversion and abuse of diplomacy; for
the constant maneuvering for position with each side seeking
victory at the expense of the other, plus the posing of rigid
demands backed by positions of strength, adds to the climate
of hostility and increases rather than reduces the possibility
of war.[16] Such diplomacy literally manufactures more obstacles to the settlement of differences.

The contemporary practice that Nehru has opposed the
most is diplomacy by condemnation and name calling. He
has agreed that it is difficult to refrain from criticizing the
policies of other states and their statesmen, for their behavior is unquestionably sometimes offensive and aggressive.
But he argues further that even when a state deserves condemnation, public attacks upon it serve only to arouse passions and tensions, push logic and reason further out of the
picture, and make the solution of the dispute more difficult.
The "habit of being moderate in language," a habit Gandhi
carefully cultivated in the Indian movement, should, therefore, become characteristic of diplomacy, for surely a name-
calling and accusation-hurling contest will not promote
peace.[17] Thus Nehru opposed the branding of Red China
as an "aggressor" by the United Nations for fear it would

further embitter Red China and make a settlement of the
Korean War by negotiation more difficult.[18]

Here it can be argued that Nehru has not always practiced what he has preached, for India has often demanded
that the UN should declare Pakistan to be an "aggressor"
in Kashmir. In branding South Africa's racial policies "per-
nicious" and "insulting," moreover, he confessed frankly
that on that subject he was not capable of the self-restraint
he ordinarily demanded of statesmen.[19]

There is no doubt, however, about Nehru's theoretical
position. He is unalterably opposed to the thesis of John
Foster Dulles, who argued that there should be more rather
than less condemnation of international wrongdoing. For to
Nehru what is "wrong-doing" to one state is "right-doing"
to another state; even war and imperialism have not been
without defenders who believed sincerely that such things
were morally justifiable. What makes name-calling and condemnation so bad, however, is the fact that such tactics
make agreement between disputants more difficult; they
make a rational and calm discussion of an issue virtually
impossible, and are, therefore, of no practical value, but are
rather an obstacle to the achievement of international
settlements.

Nehru is quick to add, however, that a friendly approach
requires something more than sweet talk. It requires also
friendly deeds. As important as the verbal approach is, Nehru
insists that a nation's friendliness can be verified only by its
behavior. It is impossible to know with any high degree of
certainty whether or not statesmen are sincere in what they
say. It is impossible to look into their hearts and heads and
discover their real motives. It is what a state actually does,
therefore, that is the final test of its friendliness or unfriend-
liness. Merely to refrain from condemnation and insult is
not enough.[20]

Nehru is equally opposed to attempts to solve international

problems by military means. Here again is an evil method that produces only evil results. Neither war nor the threat of war will produce the kind of world most men want, he has insisted; and he seems convinced that the military method has never yet solved a major world problem. Even military defense against invaders, as necessary and justifiable as it might be, brings in its wake a host of new problems and produces the risk that even the defenders will become corrupted and develop a military outlook. This is precisely what happened in the Korean War. The UN was justified, he thought, in defending South Korea and pushing back the North Korean invaders into their own territory above the 38th parallel. At that point the fighting should have been stopped and the remaining problems settled by negotiation. The tragedy was that military thinking had assumed control. It was decided, therefore, that the unification of all Korea—the major remaining problem—could best be achieved by the military method. But the UN failed completely in this objective because it used the wrong method.[21]

Nehru has confessed that his belief that war and other military methods are not suitable to the handling of many problems has been influenced largely by India's success in the use of non-violent methods. He appears to think, moreover, that the increased emphasis by the West on military methods since World War II is due in part at least to fear that any other method will be equivalent to appeasement or to a surrender to an opponent's ideology. But the militaristic approach to problems has too many weaknesses, in his view, to be used for any purpose but self-defense. In the first place, it produces a vicious circle, for its application by one party in a dispute automatically provokes the other party to use it also— and here you have the cause of the armaments races. Also war is too destructive, particularly now that nuclear weapons are available. Like so many others, Nehru has predicted that if there is a nuclear war it will result in the complete destruction of civilization. Nehru objects also to the use of war in settling disputes because it is so hard to control. Although wars are fought to attain certain objectives, too often those objectives are lost sight of as the conflict progresses and human passions intensify; and when the war is over it is discovered too late that the objectives of the war have not been attained at all. This is likely to be the case in a nuclear war since the nuclear weapons are so destructive that the objectives themselves might be destroyed. Worst of all, the application of the military approach to problems creates an undesirable psychological climate, a climate of opinion that puts emphasis on preparations for war and that gets in the way of calm, deliberate, and frank negotiation and conciliation.[22]

Another wrong method or wrong approach to international problems, in Nehru's view, is the use of pacts and alliances. He has agreed that there are occasional circumstances in which a state's security is so clearly threatened that there is justification in seeking an ally. He has agreed also that in wartime alliances are both essential and probably inevitable. But in peacetime most alliances and pacts have proved, he seems to believe, to be either worthless or downright harmful. A major trouble with them is that they are generally organized against some particular enemy or potential enemy and their very creation automatically declares that a particular state is an enemy; and this automatically promotes a hostile atmosphere. Another major objection is that pacts and alliances do little or nothing to cure the disease that produced the original hostility. He noted in the early thirties, for example, that all the post-World War I pacts such as the Washington Naval Agreement of 1922, the Locarno Pacts, the Kellogg-Briand Pact, and the Anglo-French Naval Agreement of 1928 were "desperate attempts to steady a quarrelsome and collapsing world as if such pacts or patchwork on the surface could remedy a deep-seated disease."

The deep-seated disease to him at that time was the struggle for power that was going on between the "satisfied Powers and the unsatisfied Powers," and he could not see how the pacts could do any good in resolving that struggle, for they were designed to freeze the *status quo* rather than bring about a distribution of the world's goods and power that would be acceptable to all. A generation later he was opposing the Baghdad Pact on much the same grounds—that its objectives could not be achieved by it. The Baghdad Pact, he claimed, had been designed to keep Russia out of the Middle East. In reality it had produced the opposite result, provoking Russia into taking more interest in the Middle East than ever before.[23]

Another objection to pacts and alliances, in Nehru's view, is that they often create hostile divisions among hitherto friendly states. The mere joining an alliance by one state, for example, often causes neighboring states to suspect that the alliance might someday be turned against them. The Southeast Asia Treaty, for example, to which some states of southeast Asia adhered while others did not, disturbed the stability and friendly atmosphere of the whole area, Nehru asserted. The Baghdad Pact also caused hostile divisions throughout the Middle East.[24]

A further objection to alliances is that they increase the danger of local wars expanding into world wars, for the obligation of each signatory to come to the others' aid draws states into a conflict often far removed from a merely local dispute that should be restricted to local limits.[25]

Nehru also seems to feel that alliances contain tendencies to develop in directions they were not originally intended to go and that some of these directions might not be desirable. Although the North Atlantic Treaty Organization, the Southeast Asia Treaty Organization, and the United States-Pakistan alliance were designed, for example, to stem the post-World War II tide of Communism, Nehru long harbored a suspicion that the agreements might someday be interpreted to strengthen or re-introduce colonialism in Asia and Africa. The North Atlantic Treaty in particular seemed to contain the seed of the idea that European colonial powers might someday invoke the treaty to attain NATO intervention in behalf of its members' efforts to hang on to their Afro-Asian possessions and thus perpetuate the hatred and out-worn institution of imperialism. Thus NATO had degenerated, he declared in 1952, from a defensive alliance into a pact for the defense of colonialism; and to him that was an evil development.[26]

Alliances and pacts are also flimsy and ephemeral things, in Nehru's view, which promise security for hardly more than a day. This is due to the fact that the members of alliances, especially the Great Powers, are in the habit of constantly shifting their allegiances from one side to the other. They are allies one day and enemies the next, or enemies one day and allies the next. Hitler and Stalin were enemies one day, for example; then in 1939 they became allies; and finally in mid-1941 they became enemies again. That has been going on throughout the history of international relations; and it scarcely justifies states putting more than a thimbleful of confidence in the scraps of paper so solemnly signed.[27]

Nehru has opposed some of the pacts and alliances signed since World War II not only on principle but on the grounds of Indian national interests as well. Since all the major alliances of the period were part and parcel of the cold war, Nehru turned hostile to them automatically whenever a near neighbor became involved in one of them; for Nehru was convinced that such involvement by a neighbor in the cold war would of necessity bring the cold war too close to India and disturb the so-called "area of peace" which he had so long dreamed of building among non-aligned states in the area.[28]

It must be remembered that in all this opposition to

pacts and alliances Nehru is opposed only to those that are organized *against* someone or something; he is opposed only to organizations based on assumptions of hostility. Regional or any other kinds of organizations among states designed to further cooperation and untainted with the psychological factors of fear and animosity are not only acceptable but even desirable to Nehru. For many years, in fact, Nehru gave much thought to the possibility of an organization of the states of Asia and Southeast Asia modeled along the lines of the Inter-American system. He preferred a universal organization like the UN, but he abandoned the idea completely when he became convinced there was not sufficient agreement among the states of the Asian area to sustain such an organization.[29] At all times, however, he continued to believe that organizations of states were not nearly so important as the psychological climate among them, and it was this climate that most pacts and alliances tended to worsen.

Nehru's reasons for opposing India's alignment with one of the blocs engaged in the cold war are virtually endless. In the first place, non-alignment might make it possible for India to remain outside the mainstream of big-power rivalry. Although quite conscious of the interdependence of all states, he seems to have felt that there are varying degrees of inter-dependence and involvement and that it is within the power of at least nations favorably situated geographically to avoid the inner currents of big-power hatred, jealousy, and maneuvering. The Scandinavian states had succeeded in doing that to a large extent, he noted in the early thirties, and this circumstance had had much to do with allowing the Scandinavian states to live a peaceful life and devote their energies to civilized pursuits. The United States also did this very same thing in the years of her infancy as a nation. Throughout the French Revolution and the Napoleonic Wars and their aftermath the United States avoided involvement despite her sympathies and despite the fact that all the conflicts going on within the Western world had some effect on her. Thus staying outside power blocs was a "natural policy" for a state that had recently attained her freedom, and even though the international situation today is not the same as it was in the days of George Washington, Nehru believes India should give the policy a try.[30]

A closely related reason for non-alignment is that such a policy might make it possible for India to avoid being drawn into what Nehru has referred to many times as Europe's "legacy of conflict." Although Nehru seems to have been aware always that power politics is a universal phenomenon, he has long felt that only in Europe has power politics been elevated into a political way of life supported by elaborate theories to justify it; and the result is that although all states occasionally have quarrels with their neighbors, there is nowhere else anything like the historical habit of conflict that has persisted in Europe; there is nowhere else the centuries old climate of hostility that has dominated Europe's interstate relations and that has been accentuated in the twentieth century by the unusually desperate efforts of European states to hang on to the power that is inevitably slipping away from them. Again, despite his awareness of the interdependence of states, Nehru feels that Asian states like India are only secondarily affected by European power politics and should remain out of the main stream of them as much as possible. The major problems of India and all other Asian states are about food, clothing, health, education, housing, and so on, and attention to such problems is bound to suffer if Asian nations become entangled in the European whirlpool.[31]

Nehru has defended his non-alignment policy also on the grounds of opportunism, holding that to tie a state to a bloc deprives it of freedom of maneuver, deprives it of freedom to decide future issues on the grounds of national interest and to side with whichever state or states the best interests of the nation at that future moment might demand. Even siding with an imperialist power on some future issue might, under the circumstances, be the lesser of two evils, he has claimed; and he wants India to remain in a position to do what is most opportune. Alignment with a particular bloc, more-over, obliges a state to put all one's "eggs in one basket," he has declared, and that is a risky venture.[32]

Nehru has argued also that India disagrees with the views of both the East and West blocs of the cold war on too many vital issues to allow honest alignment with either of them.[33]

Nehru has argued further that India's alignment with a bloc would not help either India or the bloc she joined enough to make it worthwhile. He seems to feel that minor powers have aligned themselves with the super-powers in the cold war not because their vital national interests required alignment but largely to gain the favor of the super-powers, largely "in the hope that some crumbs might fall from their table." And Nehru is not interested in a few crumbs. Nor does he think that minor allies are of much value to the super-powers. Rather they are burdens on the great powers. The great powers must protect and arm their minor allies, and even if the minor ally provides military bases a few hundred miles closer to the super-power's adversary, the bases are diffcult to defend and their value in a day of long-distance weapons is questionable.[34]

If it is protection against invasion that the super-powers have to offer their minor allies, India can provide her own protection, Nehru argues. He has admitted readily that India has no means of defending herself "at a dis-tance," no means of fighting abroad as demanded by the old Bismarckian dictum that a state should consider her frontiers as far away and be prepared to defend them many miles beyond her own borders. As we have already noticed, in fact, Nehru sneers at this Bismarckian (or F. D. Rooseveltian) concept of defense at a distance, arguing that to carry it out requires intervention in other states and that to engage in that justifies other states in intervening in every state. Nehru dismisses Bismarck, indeed, with the charge that the Iron Chancellor had the outlook of a European imperialist out to carve up the world and his ideas are now outmoded.[35]

But Nehru has the utmost confidence in the ability of India to defend herself *within her own borders*. Even though other states may be more powerful militarily, India has at least enough power to make a potential invader think twice as to whether or not an invasion would be worthwhile. Here India's military capacity is only one of many factors. More important is the will of her hundreds of millions of people, every man, woman, and child of whom Nehru seems to think can be mobilized in one way or another, to make life miserable and even deadly for any invader no matter how numerous or how well armed. Weak as India might be for defense beyond her borders, therefore, her defensive powers within her borders are enormous, and the protection of a great power ally is not needed.[36]

Nehru has defended his non-alignment policy also on the ground that it is only by means of such a policy that it is possible for India to influence other states, especially her neighbors. So long as she remains unaligned India can maintain a position of disinterestedness; she can assess issues on their merits; she can preserve her individuality; she can remain free of suspicion that she is an accomplice; she can serve as a conciliator and exert influence. But the moment she becomes aligned she will lose all those characteristics. Then she will become a mere reflex of another state's will, and her influence will disappear. So it is best for the whole world, Nehru has explained, that India stay out of blocs, because the need of disinterested conciliators and non-partisan influences is desperate.[37]

A final Nehru argument in favor of remaining outside the cold war blocs is that none of the great powers of recent times has had foreign policies worth following; none has had foreign policies that can be deemed successful according to Nehru's criteria of success. It must be said here, however, that Nehru is applying a criterion of success that none of the great powers has tried to meet. To Nehru a successful foreign policy has been one that succeeded in preventing a third world war and moving the world toward peace.[38] Its major objective must be peace. But it is patent that peace has been only a secondary objective of the major powers since World War II. Russia's chief goal appears to have been the expansion of Communism and Soviet power. The primary aim of the United States has been to contain the spread of Communism and Soviet power. The paramount ends of Great Britain and France have been to hang on to their positions of power and prestige. In no case has the peace Nehru believed should be put first actually been put first, despite the fact that every one of the major powers has preferred to achieve its aims by peaceful procedures.

But Nehru has made it clear on many occasions that peace is the number one need of India and all other similarly under-developed states, and a bloc of powers that does not have peace as the supreme objective of its foreign policy is not worthy to be followed.

The scientific and industrial revolutions of the past two centuries, Nehru holds, have at last opened new vistas for mankind by making it technologically possible for all men, women, and children of the globe to prosper and attain decent standards of living. But to do this the resources of the world must be used for the betterment of mankind instead of being chewed up and dissipated in war and preparation for war. To achieve these results also, the development plans and projects of the nations of the world, and particularly of the under-developed nations, must not be interfered with by quarrels and violence. Indeed war might very well destroy everything at the very threshold of humanity's greatest triumph. Thus peace should be the most important objective for every foreign policy in the present era, and the fact that it is not the paramount objective of the superpowers bars Nehru from following them.[39]

In the kind of world Nehru wants, indeed, there would be no blocs; rather there would be such a widespread dispersion of power that all possibility of a nation or group of nations dominating another would disappear.

Although he has not talked a great deal about the dispersion of power, he seems aware that here he is at grips with one of the basic issues of modern society. As he has looked at the internal affairs of nations he has observed that one of the central problems of our time is how to balance individual freedom with the technological necessity for centralization. He knows that the efficient use of a nation's resources and her technological development require a centralized direction and, therefore, a considerable centralization of power. Yet this centralization is dangerous. For it provides a reservoir of power that will almost inevitably be used by whatever group gets hold of it to impose that group's will on others. It is not only anti-social groups like fascists who will so use this power if they get hold of it. "Good crusading elements" are equally incapable of resisting the temptation to use it. The concentration of power, therefore, is a major obstacle to the broad toleration Nehru wants. The preferred course is to disperse power throughout society so that the possibility of domination is diminished. Dispersion of power will limit the temptation to dominate or will at least make the temptation manageable. For tolerance and non-domination can be assured only when conditions are such that domination is impossible and one has little choice but to tolerate what one opposes.[40]

The same principle should be applied in international affairs, Nehru thinks. Pacts, alliances, the organization of blocs, and so on, naturally concentrate power and thereby increase the temptation of each bloc to impose its will on others. If, however, the allies of the super-powers would drift away and become neutral like India, the super-powers would find themselves in a situation in which they would be forced to tolerate each other and use a peaceful approach toward each other. Without reliable allies they would have to call off the cold war and learn to co-exist peacefully.[41]

Some dispersion of power is already taking place, Nehru thinks. The rise of nationalism and the consequent popular reaction against foreign domination has already made it more difficult for the great powers to impose their will in many parts of the world where heretofore their will found few obstacles. This is especially true in Asia. There the power of the West to impose its will has been weakened also by the decline in power of the old ruling cliques that so long worked in cahoots with Western imperialists. Therefore, while the Western states are still vastly more powerful than the states of Asia, they are no longer powerful enough to have their own way. The psychological revolution among Asian peoples has mobilized a vast capacity of resistance to outside control, and this is a situation that should be promoted everywhere.[42]

What Nehru has long wanted to bring into being is what he has called a "peace area," an informal grouping of friendly, cooperative, understanding states bound together not by treaty but by a sheer desire for peace. Being opposed to blocs, the "peace area" or "no war area," as he has called it also, would not be a formally organized grouping. Rather it would be simply as many states as possible dedicated to using their influence to maintain peace, and in the event a war broke out, dedicated to using their influence for a return to peace. It could be promoted through conversations in the United Nations or outside it and would operate (supposedly in much the way an informal grouping like the Afro-Asian bloc operates within the UN) by caucuses and informal types of diplomatic contact.[43]

Here again Nehru's obsession with the psychological climate is evident, for he appears utterly uninterested in the structural arrangements through which such a group of states would cooperate, believing apparently that all that is necessary for a maximum of effectiveness is the right spirit, the proper dedication, the essential urge and will toward peace.

It must be understood clearly that in all his condemnation of pacts, alliances, and formally organized blocs Nehru is not asking any nation to be neutral on international issues. All he is asking is that a nation get out or stay out of formal groupings that are organized *against* other states or groupings of states. He expects not only India but all other states to take sides on issues that arise. The concept of neutrality is, in his view, an outmoded concept in the twentieth century. Guarantees of neutrality by the great powers, such as that long applied to Switzerland, are meaningless today, he has asserted; for there is no longer any way to keep war out of a country if one of the combatants considers it advantageous to intrude. In the event of a third world war in particular such a guarantee would be useless and even India might be forced in. Nehru has declared that in the event of such a war he would attempt to keep India out of it as long as possible, working meanwhile to stop the violence. But in the interdependent world of the twentieth century such a course would be very difficult if not impossible.[44]

What Nehru is requesting is that states remain independent, not neutral; and he is asking also that they remain outside groupings based on a climate of hostility toward other states. International organizations like the UN, the Commonwealth of Nations, or the Inter-American system based essentially on a spirit of friendly cooperation and devoid of antagonism toward other states are acceptable and desirable, in Nehru's view, and they are not to be confused with such alliances as the Warsaw Pact, NATO, SEATO, and the Baghdad Pact that can survive only so long as a spirit of fear of and hatred against other states is kept alive.

Thus pacts and alliances organized against other states, essential as they might be in rare cases, are not only obstacles to the development of the proper psychological climate among states; they actually promote a climate of hostility. They are, therefore, a wrong means, an improper method to promote a better world; and being wrong means, only undesirable results can flow from them.

The UN also would become a generator of a climate of hostility, thinks Nehru, if it should fall under the control of a particular bloc and then be used as an instrument *against* other states or *against* a bloc. Therefore Nehru is a staunch defender of the right of veto in the Security Council, abused as it might be, on the grounds that it is the chief obstacle to the prevention of the Security Council's falling under the control of one bloc. He considers the veto desirable also because it prevents the UN so often from resorting to the undesirable method of violence, and forces the UN to rely on peaceful procedures to settle disputes. When in 1950 the General Assembly took upon itself a larger role in handling threats to the peace, through the so-called Uniting for Peace Resolution, Nehru opposed the movement on the grounds that it was an attempt of one bloc in the cold war to get control of the security powers of the UN and use those powers to the bloc's advantage against another bloc. It was an attempt by one group of states to create a situation in which it could gain a victory over another group of states. Clearly this was no way to reduce tensions, abolish fear, promote friendliness, or arrive at solutions to a dispute satisfactory to all and in which all would be winners and none losers.[45]

Justified as the UN was in using military force to drive the North Koreans out of South Korea, once that was done there was no longer any justification for continuing to use a method that generated hostility and that aimed at one side achieving victory over the other side. The justifiable use of guns should never for a moment have put an end to an emphasis on and a continuation of non-violent methods to settle the dispute, of methods that do not promote hostility. Throughout the period of military operations all the parties to the dispute should have remained in communication, with Red China being seated in the Security Council; and a rational discussion of the dispute should have been pursued. The search for the truth should have been continuous.[46]

But how can there be a rational discussion among all parties to a Far Eastern problem, Nehru asks, if a great power of the Far East (Red China) is not there? In such an event, Nehru has pointed out, one-quarter of the world "is just not there"; and regardless of one's like or dislike of Communist China, her forced absence from the UN forbids an effective search for the truth and prevents the attainment of decisions voluntarily acceptable to all.[47]

The kind of diplomacy Nehru would like to see used to bring about a new civilization and a new system of international relations would be both informal and personal, very much in accord with the kind of diplomacy wanted and practiced by Franklin D. Roosevelt. Like Roosevelt, Nehru believes that national leaders should be informally in touch with each other all the time, even during the heat of disputes. Lines of communication should never be cut. Leaders should meet each other face to face as often as possible, not

in large international formal conferences, with agendas,
protocol, or secretaries, but in small informal conferences
from which they can get not only each other's frank views,
but the *feel* of each other's attitudes as well. The atmosphere
of informality and frankness of the Commonwealth conferences is one of the great merits of the Commonwealth system,
Nehru thinks. At Commonwealth meetings a variety of
views and approaches is always visible. But the atmosphere
is such that all participants are able to speak freely and
honestly and it is possible, therefore, to transmit to each
other a great deal of the *feel* of the forces and the emotions
at work in the various countries—something that cannot be
grasped in large formal international conferences open to all
the channels of publicity and in which statesmen are forbidden too often to express themselves frankly.[48]

This does not mean, Nehru has explained, that he wants
to go back to the personal and secret diplomacy of former
times which had so much evil in it. But it does mean, he has
agreed, that he would utilize the good techniques of the old
diplomacy, a diplomacy which he insists had, for all its evil,
"some finesse" and "some intelligence" about it, both of
which are lacking in the open or popular diplomacy of today.
Much of the material of diplomacy is too confidential for
public discussion.[49] Moreover, according to Gandhian philosophy every negotiation must be a search for the truth, by
all parties; and in this search for a true solution to a dispute absolute honesty and frankness must prevail. Holding
back anything in secret is forbidden. And it is obvious that if
statesmen are to discuss their disputes in the candid manner
here required, they must be allowed the privacy essential
to it.

It cannot be emphasized too much that the primary purpose of such meetings, according to Nehru, is to provide
statesmen with a continuous medium through which they
can reason together, get a clear grasp of each others' point of

view, persuade each other of the rightness or wrongness of a particular view, and change each others' minds. They are to be mediums to facilitate the search for the truth. They are not, as they were to Franklin Roosevelt, essentially meetings to allow statesmen to get to know one another and become friends on the grounds that you cannot hate a person you know well. For Nehru is convinced that it is quite possible to hate people you know and that very often getting to know one another by itself often produces dislike of one another. Even neighbors who know one another very well often rub each other the wrong way. Thus to Nehru a mere "exchange of persons" program or a program to promote cultural understanding might actually promote more quarrels, for it is self-evident to Nehru that often those "who know one another most, quarrel most." This means that the psychological attitudes taken into a meeting or infused into an international-understanding program must be of a particular kind. They must be attitudes of friendliness—on at least one side—and they must be attitudes in which the "right" kind of knowledge is exchanged, knowledge that will produce more friendliness rather than just any kind of knowledge or knowledge that will produce fear, intolerance, and an increase of tension.[50]

Thus we see that throughout virtually everything Nehru has had to say regarding international relations over a long period of years there runs the constant reiteration that all that is to be done is dependent on the psychological approach, on the means, on the method—and little else matters. He does not believe, for example, that adherence to opposing ideologies is an obstacle to international agreement so long as the parties have the proper spirit and use the proper methods in their search for a settlement. Even in the cold war, he has maintained, the issue of Communism versus anti-Communism has little bearing on the dispute and persons who persist in thinking in such ideological terms are not likely to get far. The cold war is, in his view, essentially a struggle for power between two super-powers and their allies and he doubts that the situation would be greatly different if there were no ideological differences.[51]

Chapter VII

Conclusions

IT SEEMS JUSTIFIABLE to conclude that although Nehru has provided the guiding hand for the foreign policy of his Congress Party for nearly forty years and for the independent state of India for fourteen years he has made no attempt to develop systematically a coherent and comprehensive theory of international relations. However, an attempt to summarize Nehru's thoughts reveals that he has developed three ultimate objectives.

First, he wants a world in which every man, woman, and child would have a decent material standard of living. It need be only a modest standard rather than a luxurious one, but the abject poverty, physical misery, and starvation that have so long beset the masses of mankind would be existent no longer. His goal is to wipe poverty from the face of the earth.

Second, he wants a world in which every individual, race, and nation would have equal opportunity to develop a "good" life. The domination and exploitation of one people by another would be gone. Man-made barriers to occupations or to as much education as a person can absorb would be things of the past. Man-made obstacles to a nation developing as far as it could go and in the direction it wished to go, provided it did not harm others, would be nonexistent. His goal is implementation of the age-old but never-fulfilled principle that all men are created equal. His corollary is that all nations also are equal, not in power, but in the right to opportunity to develop.

Third, he wants a world in which every individual would be able to enjoy the basic human freedoms—especially the freedoms of self-expression and self-development. It would not be a world of license, of *laissez-faire*. In the complex cultures of our time in which a certain amount of governmental centralization is needed for an efficient economy there would have to be restraints on the individual. But they would be only the restraints already considered reasonable by the Western mind. Police-state dictatorships and excessive demands for conformity associated throughout the ages with authoritarianism would be relegated to the ash heaps of history.

Obviously, there is nothing unique about these objectives. All of them are today the avowed objectives of a large portion of mankind. So compelling has the demand become that society move toward them that even those who are opposed are often forced to pay lip-service in order to retain positions of leadership.

But these objectives are not the most important part of Nehru's thinking about international relations. He is quite ready to admit that they are not everyone's objectives and that those who disagree with him have, within limits, every right to do so. Distasteful as dictatorship is to him, for example, he is the first to insist that if other people prefer it, that is their business. The only thing they do not have the right to do is impose it on others.

Nehru is also aware that regardless of his own personal desires, the world is going to remain pluralistic for the foreseeable future. Free societies and dictatorships are going to have to live side by side. Vast differences in culture are going to persist. None of the goals he seeks are going to be reached in his lifetime and all that can be asked by a reasonable man is that some progress be made toward them.

Far more important than his objectives, therefore, are those conditions and processes that are essential to allowing men to live together in a civilized fashion while working toward whatever objectives they happen to have. His overriding concern is with the conditions and processes that will allow men to live and let others live regardless of what their objectives are now or what they might be in the future.

Nehru knows that men's ends form a complex and ever shifting hierarchy, with many goals being merely stepping stones to other goals. Men disagree, moreover, as to what ends are socially justifiable. There is continuous conflict about them. Human life cannot possibly be uniformly tranquil and harmonious. It is inevitable that problems shall litter the path of every human being, of every social group, of every nation. Life is an obstacle course for both men and states. And those who believe the course can be cleared and transformed into an idyllic road are nothing less than wishful-thinking utopians.

It is how men go about traversing the road of life that is all important. The mental attitudes they bring to the task can make the journey easier or harder. The social, economic, and political institutions or systems they develop along the way can help surmount obstacles or create additional obstacles. The methods they apply can prevent tragedy or produce unnecessary tragedy.

These mental attitudes, these institutions or systems, and these methods are all, in Nehru's view, man-made; or if, as in the case of the attitude of fear, they are not man-made, they are at least susceptible to man's control. Religious intolerance is a learned attitude; war is a man-made institution; a diplomacy of condemnation is a humanly contrived method. They are neither part of a divine plan nor inherent in the nature of man or society. They are the results of the workings of human minds and wills. In some cases they are the results of the systems, ideologies, or institutions that have grown up, such as feudalism, imperialism, capitalism, and so on. But these systems too are man-made; and when they are changed or abolished, the attitudes and ways of behaving that are part and parcel of them will be changed or abolished also.

Thus far in history, Nehru holds, men have not made a very admirable record in developing the best possible attitudes, institutions, and methods. They have had some success, to be sure. The desirable attitude of tolerance has been cultivated to a degree. Some splendid systems, such as democracy, and some useful institutions, such as the United Nations, have been produced. Some excellent methods of attacking problems, such as the empirical method, have been developed.

But on the whole the attitudes, systems, and methods men have applied to their struggle to traverse the obstacle-strewn road of life have not been by any means the best the human mind and will can devise. Many methods that were useful to meet conditions in a former time, moreover, have been retained and even hallowed long after their usefulness has come to an end. Many that were once good and useful were also later corrupted and were transformed into attitudes, institutions, and methods that became harmful.

The psychological attitudes that Nehru believes have been the greatest obstacles to man's progress are fear, intolerance, dogmatism, hostility, excessive acquisitiveness, and feelings of superiority. In more recent times the attitude of nationalism has developed excessively and has also become a major cause of harm. By exploiting such attitudes among the masses of mankind, a minority of every society and a minority of states have been successful in developing a "good" life and in traversing the obstacle course of life with relative ease. But the vast majority of mankind has remained wretched. The minority has attained the "good" life and has successfully traveled the road of life largely by riding on the backs or walking over the prostrate bodies of the many.

Among the institutions or systems that have made life worse for most men than it need be, the major ones that Nehru looks upon as all bad are war, imperialism, hierarchical class or caste systems, and aggressive-violent systems like fascism. Many others once were good but were perverted or became useless as new conditions developed. The independent, sovereign national state was a useful institution for some time and has only recently become outmoded because of ever increasing interdependence. All the great religions were good and useful in developing and disseminating moral codes, but virtually all of them have been corrupted and in their corrupt form they have promoted superstition, intolerance, dogmatism, fear, excessive conservatism, violence, and other obstacles to progress. Capitalism once also made great contributions to society but in its *laissez-faire* form it outlived its usefulness and in some respects actually promoted poverty, war, imperialism, and other forms of human misery. In its goals and ideals Communism has been a great advance over capitalism, but its methods have been a source of incalculable suffering.

The methods men have applied in the attempt to overcome the obstacles they encounter have also too often been, in Nehru's view, the wrong methods. Methods of force and violence, of crusading, of condemnation, of organizing hostile alliances, the whole complex of methods implied in the term authoritarianism, and the whole complex of methods implied in the term power politics have been wrong methods.

The most amazing thing to Nehru is that mankind has survived in spite of its often inept struggle to surmount the many natural obstacles. And it is this capacity for endurance and persistence in the nature of man that is the chief source of Nehru's optimism about the future. That he is optimistic without being utopian is obvious. He believes with the profound conviction characteristic of all reformers that the psychological attitudes, the institutions, and the methods that are not now desirable or useful can be abolished or transformed to at least a considerable degree and be replaced with attitudes, institutions, and methods that will at least approximate a "good" life for most men. His confidence in the mind and will of man is very great. There is a stout faith in his heart that life can be made better than it has ever been before. Unlike many religious leaders he promises no eternal heaven or nirvana. Unlike some Marxists, he promises no earthly utopia. All he promises are better conditions and processes for surmounting inevitable obstacles.

The psychological attitudes Nehru looks upon as prerequisite to a better civilization are many and varied. He wants the "new man" of the new civilization to be fearless, rational, tolerant, friendly, cooperative, equalitarian, self-reliant, internationalist, and no more than modestly acquisitive; and he wants those attitudes reflected in the foreign policies of the nations.

Of new institutions he seems to propose only two: a welfare state (not now so new) and an eventual world federation.

The methods to be used for the tackling of problems and the settling of conflicts are to be non-violent, democratic, non-crusading procedures of accommodation that will allow the reality of peaceful co-existence in what is inevitably to remain a pluralistic world. A club of military force may be kept behind the door, just in case; but there is little expectation, given the above prerequisites, that it will have to be used except in extremely rare instances; and even when used, the non-violent methods are to continue functioning in an effort to get the violence stopped.

In calling for such a transformation in men's attitudes, institutions, and methods Nehru is obviously calling for a great deal. And at first sight he appears utopian. He even appears naive. But it is a bit risky to call a man a naive utopian who over a period of forty years has proved himself to be a remarkably effective political leader, who has won the admiration of literally hundreds of millions of men, who has repeatedly won free elections by the rough-and-tumble democratic process, and who over a period of fourteen years has provided the most stable new government to operate via the difficult democratic process since the end of World War II. Nehru might be considered a super-realist with a keener perception of the nature of man and his social environment than is possessed by the so-called practical realist who takes a less optimistic view of what can be achieved in this imperfect world.

The truth is that we do not know and cannot know at the present time whether Nehru is a naive utopian, a super-realist, or something in between. His world view starts, as must all world views, with assumptions about the nature of man and of society, which in the present state of the social sciences can be neither proved nor disproved. Powerful arguments can be developed both for and against his position.

But whether or not the goals Nehru calls for are humanly achievable is irrelevant. It is self-evident that they are partially achievable; and we know that any degree of progress toward them will make a better world. Even if it is impossible for man to approach his social problems as fearlessly and as rationally as a scientist approaches his problems in the laboratory it is self-evident that the degree of rationalism in society can be increased. Even Machiavelli, a super-pessimist about the nature of man, seemed to believe a few leaders could be found who could be taught to direct the affairs of state in a rational manner.

Whether or not power politics is inherent in the nature of organized society or is, as Nehru holds, an ephemeral historical accident that can be totally abolished, is irrelevant also; for there is no doubt that power politics can be moderated, that the degree of hostility prevailing can be decreased, and that diplomacy of accommodation can be practiced within the general framework of power. Man's attitudes, institutions, and methods can be improved even if they cannot be perfected. Even the dismal-minded Hobbes, in a previous period of violence and anarchy, had that much hope.

Unfortunately, it will not be possible to evaluate Nehru's world view with much accuracy until much testing has been done with it, until many more experiments than his own have been made with it. Happily, experimentation with it is not dependent on its being tried by the whole world. Experimentation with such philosophies as anarchism and pacifism requires their universal acceptance, but the Nehru theory can be tried by a single nation since it makes no demand that a nation make herself physically defenseless while trying it. A stout club of military power can be kept behind the door to be used if necessary.

It can be argued further that during the experimental period the Nehru approach does not in reality forbid the use of power politics. It forbids the use of only those types of power that involve physical violence and that are unworkable without an atmosphere of hostility. All other types of power—economic, psychological, and moral—are permissible, provided they are used according to certain guiding principles such as honesty, truth, and so on. The Gandhi movement in India used a fantastic arsenal of power techniques—boycotts, strikes, civil disobedience, propaganda, jail-going, demonstrations, fasts, and every non-violent device conceivable to undermine the power of the opposition and to influence the opposition's point of view.

Nehru has made virtually no suggestions as to how such non-violent types of power can be applied in international relations, except in the anti-colonial struggle. The nearest he has come to a suggestion is his advocacy of economic sanctions to check aggressor states. And he is favorable to the application of the force of world public opinion. We know further that he is in favor of the very powerful force of example, probably in the long run the most powerful influence in society. Supposedly also, Nehru has no objection to the techniques of foreign aid and the dissemination of information to foreign peoples provided certain rules are followed. A nation experimenting with the Nehru approach would not, therefore, make herself either defenseless or unable to pursue her national interests with substantial vigor.

Such a nation would, however, have to abandon her military alliances or any alliance organized *against* another state or states. She would have to put her military club behind the door. She could keep it intact for emergency use; but she could not brandish it, as is the usual custom, to support her foreign policy. She would have to abandon also the age-old custom of keeping her own people united and loyal by portraying foreign states as predatory devils and arousing hatred against them.

Whether or not the renunciation of these traditional techniques of power politics would actually weaken a state is debatable. It seems likely that it would weaken the state's readily available military power; for it is difficult to persuade a people to support a powerful military machine unless they are told repeatedly that some foreign devil is out to get them. But since no state ever knows how much military power she might need at some future moment in some unknown circumstances to defend herself, there is no certainty that this weakening of force would be harmful.

Nehru's answer seems to go something like this: No state needs enough military power to *defeat* an attacker. All she needs is enough power, military and otherwise, to make the price of attack so high and the reward so low that attack will not be worthwhile. Assuredly, that is a debatable hypothesis; but it is unquestionably worthy of debate.

It is quite possible, as Nehru sees it, that the weakening of a state's military power might be offset automatically by the strengthening of some other forms of power. For example, it is probable that a state's moral and psychological influence would be augmented by a voluntary decrease in military might. Transferring money from military programs to economic and social-betterment programs either at home or abroad might also automatically increase her economic and social sinews as well as her economic and social influence abroad.

It is worth noting also that much of the military power now existing has proved to be useless in many situations because no one dares to use it. Since World War II there have been repeated novel exhibitions of small and backward states slapping the nuclear-armed great powers in the face and daring them to use their super-weapons—or any kind of weapons for that matter—against them. Nasser's provocations against all the great powers and Castro's provocations against the United States are but among many examples of behavior inconceivable fifty years ago. Obviously, the great new weapons are useful to their possessors for their deterrent effect on other possessors; but it is doubtful that many are needed for this purpose; and it is doubtful that they need to be brandished.

A major weakness of Nehru's theory is that it does not provide us with sufficient guidance as to how we should go about bringing into being the attitudes, institutions, and methods he advocates.

It is obvious that if the "new man" Nehru desires could be produced in sufficient numbers life for all would be much better. But that is the same as saying that if enough men could be made into good Christians, good Moslems, or good

Buddhists life for all would be vastly improved. Despite several centuries of elaborate and costly effort to make men good Christians, good Moslems, or good Buddhists only modest results have been achieved. It is also the goal of Communism to bring into being a "new man" and for more than forty years Soviet regimes have been engaged in that task, using all the instruments and techniques of totalitarianism for that purpose. Thus far, however, their progress has been disappointing even to them.

We know, of course, that the kind of men Nehru calls for can be produced. He is one himself. Doubtless there are also other men in the world who are characterized by an unusually high degree of fearlessness, rationalism, tolerance, cooperativeness, self-discipline, and so on; and more could be created. But the number of such people is small just as the number of good Christians is small.

The obstacles to the creation of Nehru's "new man" are myriad; many of them are built into society and the problem of surmounting them seems insoluble. Many individuals, organizations, and governments, for example, find it so much easier to carry out their programs by arousing fear, emotionalism, intolerance, or violence that the temptation to resort to such methods is well-nigh irresistible. Many an institution in society would wither away if its members became very rational, and it is unlikely that those who believe they benefit from such institutions would encourage the very thing that would destroy them. Many a government often finds itself so beset with insoluble problems that in order to remain in power it finds it convenient, even if not necessary, to blame foreigners for its troubles and to arouse hatred among its peoples against the aliens who, it declares, are the cause of the nation's frustrations.

Social scientists might be right in arguing that all men's social attitudes and behavior are learned and that men can be conditioned into almost any desired attitudes or behavior. It is self-evident that men can be brought to be tolerant of differing religions or intolerant of them, to believe in either the equality of man or the inequality of man, to fear change or to look forward to change, to be cooperative or competitive, and so on. But social scientists are still largely ignorant as to how psychological transformations in a whole population are brought about. Studies of past transformations reveal the factors operating in them, but reproducing those factors (such as the age of discovery of the fifteenth and sixteenth centuries) for use in the present is impossible. Indeed it is questionable whether a particularly desired psychological transformation of a whole population can be consciously achieved. The Soviet experiment might end by proving that it can be done. But virtually all other such transformations appear to have been unconscious, undirected developments that, like Topsy, "just growed." Where a strong trend has already developed, unusual personalities such as a Hitler or a Gandhi have been able to take hold of it and give it some direction; the trend toward fascism was strong in Germany before Hitler came along just as the nationalistic trend was strong in India before Gandhi appeared. Such movements are infinitely complex and it is difficult even for students of them to distinguish between underlying causes or mere superficial symptoms.

There are, to be sure, a few implications in Nehru's thinking as to how his desired psychological transformation might be achieved. He seems to think that some progress can be made by the ancient pedagogical method of verbal teaching, supplemented by example. He never tires of telling how Gandhi did away with much of the Indian peasant's fear simply by talking to him and by being fearless in his own behavior. He admits there might have been something peculiarly magnetic about the Gandhi personality that gave his quiet, school-masterish words an unusual power; and he admits also that Gandhi's exemplary behavior of fearlessness had a dramatic quality that captured the imagination of the masses as no one else in India seemed able to do. At any rate, the psychological transformation was real and it was achieved by teaching and example.

Nehru seems to feel, in fact, that arousing interest in the whole Gandhi philosophy and technique of Satyagraha contains promise of promoting the transformation he desires. Everywhere he has gone in the world since India attained her independence he has called the attention of his many audiences to the Gandhi philosophy and methodology. And thus far the results have been impressive. Scholars and social leaders interested in the problem of conflict in society have turned to a study of Gandhi's methodology in increasing numbers from many parts of the world. The literature about it is expanding rapidly and information about it is seeping into some of the world's textbooks and classrooms. Negro leaders in the United States and Africa have been particularly impressed by it; some of them have gone to India to study it; and it has already been applied to some of the Negro campaigns for equality in the southern part of the United States—notably in the campaigns to abolish racial segregation on buses in Montgomery, Alabama, in 1957 and in public eating places in 1960.

The Gandhi philosophy and technique have such obvious merits and are applicable to so many situations calling for social change that they are bound to spread; and Nehru seems hopeful that as they move some progress toward his desired attitudes and methods will be made.

Nehru implies also that many of the desired changes will come automatically as the result of forces already in motion. As such systems as imperialism and *laissez-faire* capitalism wane, for example, the undesirable attitudes of inequality and domination inherent in them might wane with them. As Communism and the new capitalism come closer together in some form of welfare statism, the hostility those systems aroused all over the world is likely to diminsh. As the Communist states become more secure, their authoritarianism is apt to fade. As the democratic process proves it can solve the basic problems of society (as Nehru believes it can) its popularity will be enhanced. As the power of military weapons becomes more horrible to contemplate, the urge to non-violence is likely to be augmented. Thus there are some forces at work in the world pushing man in the desired direction.

But these suggestions and implications for bringing about the kind of transformation Nehru wants do not look very promising to a realistic student of either history or the contemporary world. Saintly geniuses like Gandhi do not arise very often to lead people and there is little assurance that his accomplishments in India can be duplicated elsewhere. And even in India, Gandhi was unable to prevent the development of religious intolerance of an almost unprecedented depth or the carnage that accompanied partition. Since the Gandhi philosophy and methodology were developed for application *within* a state, many parts of it are not applicable to international relations. Too, Gandhism was developed to obtain changes within a relatively liberal society presided over by a relatively liberal government, the British government; and there is not much assurance that the system can be effective in a totalitarian authoritarian society. Even if the British did apply some aspects of fascism to their rule in India, as Nehru insists they did, British fascism was a far cry from Hitler's fascism or from Soviet communism.

There is little assurance, moreover, that the forces now in motion in the world will contribute much to the kind of change Nehru wants. For every desirable force there appears to be a counter force. As the Communist states become more secure there is as much chance that they will become emboldened to press on with their program of world revolution as there is that their aggressiveness will recede. Their every success is a testimonial in favor of totalitarian authoritarianism. And so it goes. The forces now in motion in the world certainly cannot be counted upon to move us toward the kind of civilization Nehru wants.

Perhaps the most difficult to accept of all Nehru's ideas is the idea that conflicts of interest can be resolved to everyone's advantage, that there need be no losers: all can win, and one's opponent should be approached in a spirit which says: "I am your friend and I'm anxious to help you; I want a solution to our dispute that will be to your advantage as well as to mine. I do not want a victory over you; and I will not accept a final decision that does not have the whole-hearted approval of both of us."

There is nothing new, of course, about the idea that there are really no basic conflicts among either individuals or states. The Stoics believed that if all individuals and states could discover their real interests they would find all were in harmony. This idea has always been central to the concept of internationalism and has been advocated by a host of political leaders—Woodrow Wilson, Franklin Roosevelt, Gandhi, and Nehru are but among the most recent. The idea that one side should not triumph over the other is, however, an idea of some novelty, and there is little historic background in any contemporary society conducive to its acceptance.

With the exception of a few rare cultures familiar only to anthropologists, all cultures have operated on the assumption that there *are* conflicts among the interests of men and states and that very often they can be resolved only by one side's triumphing over the other. Soviet Communists have made vigorous efforts to refute this contention by holding that within their socialist system conflicts of interest no longer exist; but their thesis has not appeared very convincing to anyone but themselves. Democratic societies are premised on the belief certainly that conflicts of interest are real and that elections and the legislative process are simply civilized ways whereby one side can gain a victory over the other without violence or without a decision by an arbitrary authority.

It is true that in international relations there has always been an ideal that negotiations should result in agreements mutually advantageous to all parties. But the ideal has been violated as often as it has been achieved; a large portion of the treaties made have been imposed by one side on the other; and it is fair to say that few negotiators enter international conferences with a goal of mutual advantage. Their aim is to advance the interests of their own state rather than the interests of all.

It is axiomatic in social science that effective change will occur only if the change evolves naturally out of the past experiences of people; and the Gandhi-Nehru thesis seems to have very little in the way of historical precedent.

But it would be wrong to condemn Nehru's world view simply because it appears impossible of achievement—for it might not be as impossible as it appears. Despite his many failures man has had some magnificent successes. Anti-democratic philosophers from Plato to Hobbes would be surprised at the remarkably high level of civilization attained through the democratic process by the mid-twentieth century. The United States would seem to them little short of a miracle of social and political ingenuity. The development of effective parliaments, of a workable federalism, of organized political parties, of an independent judiciary, of electoral machinery used over a vast area by great masses of people, and many other political developments testify to the fact it is not only in the natural sciences that man can be creative. Significant breakthroughs in the management of public affairs might well be achieved in the future, and they might prove that the kind of rational, tolerant, cooperative civilization Nehru wants is not impossible after all.

Notes

CHAPTER I

1. Tibor Mende, *Nehru: Conversations on India and World Affairs* (New York, 1956), 10-16.
2. *Nehru's Press Conferences, 1952* (New Delhi, Information Service of India, n. d.), 27-28.
3. Jawaharlal Nehru, *Glimpses of World History* (New York, 1942), 58.
4. *Ibid.*, 6-7, 58-59. Hereafter titles listed without an author are by Nehru.
5. See Daniel Katz and Richard L. Schanck, *Social Psychology* (New York, 1938), 153.
6. *Glimpses of World History*, 7.
7. *Ibid.*, 44, 172, 277.
8. *Ibid.*, 180-81, 277, 572.
9. *Ibid.*, 172; *The Discovery of India* (New York, 1946), 516.
10. *Glimpses of World History*, 936; *Discovery of India*, 18.
11. *Glimpses of World History*, 435; *Toward Freedom: The Autobiography of Jawaharlal Nehru* (New York, 1941), 266, 323; J. S. Bright (ed.), *Selected Writings of Jawaharlal Nehru, 1916-1950* (New Delhi, 1950), 255.
12. *Ibid.*, 59; *The Unity of India:* *Collected Writings, 1937-1940* (New York, 1942), 31; N. V. Rajkumar (ed.), *The Background of India's Foreign Policy* (New Delhi, 1952), 67.
13. *Glimpses of World History*, 182, 253; *Discovery of India*, 44-45.
14. *Ibid;* 490-91.
15. Bright, *Selected Writings of Jawaharlal Nehru*, 290-91.
16. *Ibid.*, 290-91; *Visit to America* (New York, 1950), 166, 178-80; *Unity of India*, 323-24, 327-28; Mende, *Nehru,* 17-18.
17. Frank Moraes, *Jawaharlal Nehru: A Biography* (New York, 1956), 277, 285.
18. *Jawaharlal Nehru's Speeches, 1949-53* (New Delhi, Information Service of India, 1954), 179, 187.
19. *Ibid.*, 187, 192, 375; *Vital Speeches*, December 15, 1956, p. 143.
20. *Unity of India*, 219.
21. *Unity of India*, 28; *Nehru's Speeches, 1949-53*, p. 397; Mende, *Nehru*, 100-01, 104.
22. *Ibid.*, 101.
23. *Glimpses of World History*, 932; *Visit to America*, 25-26, 109, 146; *Nehru's Speeches, 1949-53*, pp.

182-83; *Independence and After* (New York, 1950), 204; Werner Levi, *Free India in Asia* (Minneapolis, 1952), i, 49, 114-15.

24. *Glimpses of World History*, 280, 449, 611, 613, 813; *Nehru's Speeches, 1949-53*, pp. 360-61; *Toward Freedom*, 225; *Vital Speeches*, January 1, 1957, p. 170; *New York Times Magazine*, September 7, 1958, p. 13. Nehru himself is, indeed, an excellent example of this disease of "moral myopia" in international relations. His position on many issues has appeared selfrighteous; but his own behavior regarding Kashmir and Hyderabad, and his frequent condemnation of the West for behavior not condemned in the East has not contributed to his acceptance everywhere as one of Plato's all-wise philosopher-kings.

25. *Nehru's Speeches, 1949-53*, p. 17; *Independence and After*, 233-35.

26. *Ibid.*, 216.

27. *Visit to America*, 93-94.

28. *Glimpses of World History*, 476.

29. J. C. Kundra, *Indian Foreign Policy, 1947-1954* (Groningen, Netherlands, 1955), 18.

30. *Visit to America*, 121, 124-25; Mende, *Nehru*, 42.

31. *Ibid.*, 102.

32. *Ibid.*, 5; *Nehru's Speeches, 1949-53*, pp. 167, 178.

CHAPTER II

1. Michael Brecher, *Nehru: A Political Biography* (New York, 1959), 99.

2. *Glimpses of World History*, 173, 202.

3. *Ibid.*, 865; *Toward Freedom*, 229-30.

4. *Discovery of India*, 523; Bright, *Selected Writings of Jawaharlal Nehru*, 72.

5. *Discovery of India*, 525.

6. *Saturday Review of Literature*, April 14, 1951.

7. *Glimpses of World History*, 232-33.

8. *Ibid.*, 871; *Discovery of India*, 20.

9. Bright, *Selected Writings of Jawaharlal Nehru*, 110.

10. *Discovery of India*, 552-53; *Nehru's Speeches, 1949-53*, p. 365; *Visit to America*, 180.

11. *Nehru's Speeches, 1949-53*, pp. 456-57; *Toward Freedom*, 254; *Visit to America*, 167; *Nehru's Press Conferences, 1952*, p. 28.

12. *Glimpses of World History*, 128; *Unity of India*, 15.

13. *Nehru's Press Conferences, 1953*, pp. 41-42.

14. *Saturday Review of Literature*, April 14, 1951.

15. *Ibid.*, December 12, 1953; *Nehru's Speeches, 1949-53*, pp. 375, 462.

16. *Independence and After*, 251.

17. *Glimpses of World History*, 8.

18. *Unity of India*, 341; Bright, *Selected Writings of Jawaharlal Nehru*, 173.

19. *Unity of India*, 181.

20. *Visit to America*, 9.

21. *Vital Speeches*, December 15, 1956, p. 142; Brecher, *Nehru*, 30-31.

22. *Glimpses of World History*, 615; *Independence and After*, 284.

23. For illustrations of Nehru's account see *Visit to America*, 49-52, 90-94; *Nehru's Speeches, 1949-53*, pp. 112-14.

24. For the text of the resolution see Rajkumer, *Background of India's Foreign Policy*, 7. Nehru was in charge of Congress foreign policy from the inception of Congress interest in the matter and this resolution, therefore, is considered a product of his thinking.

25. *Independence and After*, 322;

Nehru's Speeches, 1949-53, pp.
190, 230; Mende, *Nehru,* 80-81.
26. *Nehru's Speeches, 1949-53,* p. 415;
Moraes, *Nehru,* 459.

27. *Nehru's Speeches, 1949-53,* pp.
166, 170-72, 190, 216-17, 248.
28. *Visit to America,* 30-31.

CHAPTER III

1. Gardner Murphy, *In the Minds
of Men* (New York, 1953), 239.
2. *Unity of India,* 16-17.
3. *Nehru's Speeches, 1949-53,* pp.
118-19, 374-75; *Independence and
After,* 275-76; *Saturday Review
of Literature,* December 12, 1953.
4. *Visit to America,* 128-30, 166.
5. *Glimpses of World History,* 9-10.
6. *Ibid.,* 401; *Discovery of India,*
42-43; *Independence and After,*
260; *Nehru's Speeches, 1949-53,*
p. 385.
7. *Visit to America,* 17.
8. Mende, *Nehru,* 93, 97-98.
9. *Vital Speeches,* January 1, 1957,
pp. 169-70.
10. Mende, *Nehru,* 101.
11. *Visit to America,* 18.
12. *Unity of India,* 164.
13. *Nehru's Press Conferences, 1953,*
pp. 70-71.
14. *Ibid.,* 71-72.
15. *Nehru's Speeches, 1949-53,* pp.
373-74; *Saturday Review of Literature,* April 21, 1951, p. 48;

Mende, *Nehru,* 74; *Nehru's Press
Conferences, 1953,* p. 78.
16. Interview in *United States News
and World Report,* September 15,
1950, p. 31. Nehru's refusal to
recognize Israel is, of course, contrary to what he has preached.
However, all it proves is that
Nehru is human enough to occasionally be inconsistent. See also *Nehru's Speeches, 1949-53,* p.
232; Karaunakar Gupta, *Indian
Foreign Policy* (Calcutta, 1956),
48; Brecher, *Nehru,* 571-72.
17. *Nehru's Speeches, 1949-53,* p. 189;
Independence and After, 241.
18. Brecher, *Nehru,* 29-30.
19. *Glimpses of World History,* 846.
20. Moraes, *Nehru,* 455, 474; Kundra,
Indian Foreign Policy, 62-63.
21. *New York Times Magazine,* Octo-
ber 4, 1959.
22. *Independence and After,* 275; *India and the United Nations* (New
York, Indian Council of World
Affairs, 1957), 56.

CHAPTER IV

1. Moraes, *Nehru,* 177-78; B. S. N.
Murti, *Nehru's Foreign Policy*
(New Delhi, 1953), 7, 38-39;
Rajkumer, *Background of India's
Foreign Policy,* 1-2.
2. *Discovery of India,* 424; Brecher,
Nehru, 107, 110-11, 616.
3. *Discovery of India,* 424-26.
4. *Ibid.,* 526-28.
5. *Nehru's Speeches, 1949-53,* pp.
163-64; Mende, *Nehru,* 59.
6. *Glimpses of World History,* 708;

Unity of India, 335; *Discovery of
India,* 41-42; *Nehru's Speeches,
1949-53,* pp. 163-64, 221, 361.
7. *Visit to America,* 39-40. The persistence of excessive nationalism
in Arab lands even after independence does not bear out Nehru's prophecy for at least those
areas. But it is possible that the
continuance of fanatical nationalism in Arab lands is due to the
fact that although imperialism

has departed from most of the area legally, many vestiges of it remain politically and economically.

8. *Independence and After*, 204-05.
9. *Ibid.*, 215.
10. *Nehru's Speeches, 1949-53*, p. 176.
11. Levi, *Free India in Asia*, 101-02.
12. Gupta, *Indian Foreign Policy*, 29, 43-44.
13. *Ibid.*, 20; *Nehru's Speeches, 1949-53*, p. 217.
14. *Discovery of India*, 553; *Independence and After*, 266.
15. *Unity of India*, 327-28; Bright, *Selected Writings of Jawaharlal Nehru*, 289.
16. *Ibid.*, 267; *Unity of India*, 273, 337-38; *Discovery of India*, 552.
17. Mende, *Nehru*, 133.
18. *Discovery of India*, 551-52.
19. *Ibid.*, 551-52.
20. *Ibid.*, 549-52; Bright, *Selected Writings of Jawaharlal Nehru*, 252-54.
21. *Independence and After*, 275; *Visit to America*, 148; *Nehru's Speeches, 1949-53*, p. 398.

22. *Press Conferences, 1953*, pp. 7, 19; *Glimpses of World History*, 4, 182; *Independence and After*, 251-52; Moraes, *Nehru*, 420.
23. *Unity of India*, 113-14, 266, 270; *Toward Freedom*, 358-59.
24. *Unity of India*, 149.
25. *Visit to America*, 83; Gupta, *Indian Foreign Policy*, 83; Levi, *Free India in Asia*, 41.
26. *Independence and After*, 304-05; *Visit to America*, 73; *Nehru's Speeches, 1949-53*, p. 386; Moraes, *Nehru*, 448.
27. *Independence and After*, 253; *Press Conferences*, 1953, p. 41.
28. *Discovery of India*, 542-44; Bright, *Selected Writings of Jawaharlal Nehru*, 274, 279; *Toward Freedom*, 365.
29. Moraes, *Nehru*, 148-49; *Glimpses of World History*, 95-96.
30. *Unity of India*, 217, 272-73; *Independence and After*, 299; Moraes, *Nehru*, 448.
31. *Discovery of India*, 544; *Toward Freedom*, 373; *Independence and After*, 303; *Visit to America*, 87-88.

CHAPTER V

1. *Discovery of India*, 570.
2. Mende, *Nehru*, 44-45; Brecher, *Nehru*, 195.
3. *Glimpses of World History*, 609.
4. *Ibid.*, 59.
5. *Ibid.*, 686-87.
6. *Ibid.*, 354, 687, 875-82; *Toward Freedom*, 345.
7. *Glimpses of World History*, 33, 404, 801-02.
8. *Toward Freedom*, 324; *Unity of India*, 117-19.
9. *Glimpses of World History*, 608; Moraes, *Nehru*, 421, 439.
10. *Ibid.*, 402, 801-03, 873, 875-906.
11. *Glimpses of World History*, 96, 395, 399, 459, 478-79, 569-71, 667-74.

12. *Discovery of India*, 518; *Unity of India*, 12; *Visit to America*, 120. This thesis is questionable. Although Thailand remained independent she remained as underdeveloped as her colonially-controlled neighbors. In Africa, moreover, the two territories that remained independent throughout virtually all the recent imperialistic movement — Ethiopia and Liberia — have shown less progress toward modernization than the areas that became colonies.
13. *Independence and After*, 289; *Nehru's Speeches, 1949-53*, p. 214.
14. Mende, *Nehru*, 69, 133-35.

15. *Glimpses of World History,* 686-87, 836, 946-48; *Toward Freedom,* 345, 348; *Unity of India,* 117-19; interview in *U. S. News and World Report,* September 15, 1950, p. 31.
16. *Glimpses of World History,* 582, 826.
17. *Toward Freedom,* 392-94, 416, 418-19; *Unity of India,* 35-36.
18. *Glimpses of World History,* 955-57, 960; *Unity of India,* 149.
19. *Discovery of India,* 6-7, 424.
20. Kundra, *Indian Foreign Policy,* 28; *Unity of India,* 268; *Glimpses of World History,* 625.
21. *Ibid.,* 502.
22. *Unity of India,* 268, 284-87, 302-03, 311-12.
23. *New York Times Magazine,* September 7, 1958.
24. *Nehru's Press Conferences, 1952,* pp. 227-28; Brecher, *Nehru,* 604.
25. *New York Times Magazine,* March 11, 1956, p. 13.
26. *Glimpses of World History,* 836; interview in *U. S. News and World Report,* September 15, 1950, p. 31; Mende, *Nehru,* 94-95.
27. *New York Times Magazine,* September 7, 1958, p. 111.
28. Chester Bowles, *Ambassador's Report* (New York, 1954), 106. See also Mende, *Nehru,* 93-94; Brecher, *Nehru,* Chapter XVIII.
29. *New York Times Magazine,* September 7, 1958, p. 111.
30. *Unity of India,* 11; Bright, *Se-lected Writings of Jawaharlal Nehru,* 71; *Visit to America,* 96-97, 121; Mende, *Nehru,* 99-118; Brecher, *Nehru,* 419-20.
31. Brecher, *Nehru,* 253.
32. *Visit to America,* 123.
33. *Glimpses of World History,* 232.
34. *Unity of India,* 181; *Visit to America,* 136.
35. *Unity of India,* 67-69.
36. *Glimpses of World History,* 529, 935.
37. *Nehru's Speeches, 1949-53,* pp. 386-87.
38. *Ibid.,* 252.
39. *Ibid.,* 252, 454; interview in *Saturday Review of Literature,* April 14, 1951, p. 15.
40. Mende, *Nehru,* 48-52; Moraes, *Nehru,* 432-40; *Nehru's Speeches, 1949-53,* pp. 251-52.
41. Moraes, *Nehru,* 436.
42. Mende, *Nehru,* 65-68, 95-96; *Nehru's Speeches, 1949-53,* p. 100; *Nehru's Press Conferences, 1952,* p. 10; *Ibid.,* 1953, p. 5; *New York Times,* March 19, 1959.
43. *Glimpses of World History,* 118; *Independence and After,* 308; *Nehru's Speeches, 1949-53,* p. 100; *Visit to America,* 76-77; *Nehru's Press Conferences, 1952,* p. 10; Mende, *Nehru,* 65-68.
44. Nehru emphasized this point of view to Averell Harriman when the latter visited him in early 1959. See *New York Times,* March 19, 1959.

CHAPTER VI

1. For an excellent description and analysis of Gandhi's Satyagraha philosophy and methodology see Joan V. Bondurant, *Conquest of Violence: The Gandhian Philosophy of Conflict* (Princeton, New Jersey, 1958).
2. Mende, *Nehru,* 31; *Visit to America,* 145, 182.
3. *Independence and After,* 278, 303, 318.
4. *Nehru's Press Conferences, 1953,* pp. 44, 46.
5. Mende, *Nehru,* 140-42.

6. Bright, *Selected Writings of Jawa-harlal Nehru*, 49, 254; *Visit to America*, 90-94, 99.

7. *Nehru's Speeches, 1949-53*, pp. 396-97; *New York Times*, January 17, 1955.

8. *Visit to America*, 28-29; Bright, *Selected Writings of Jawaharlal Nehru*, 339.

9. Mende, *Nehru*, 77-78.

10. Brecher, *Nehru*, 123, 196.

11. *Nehru's Press Conferences, 1952*, p. 99; *Ibid.*, 1953, pp. 2, 16, 36; *Unity of India*, 97; Mende, *Nehru*, 79; Moraes, *Nehru*, 283, 462; Kundra, *Indian Foreign Policy*, 128.

12. *Nehru's Press Conferences, 1953*, pp. 7-8, 37-38; Mende, *Nehru*, 85-86.

13. Ross N. Berkes and Mohinder S. Bedi, *The Diplomacy of India: Indian Foreign Policy in the United Nations* (Stanford, Calif., 1958), 38.

14. Interview in *Saturday Review of Literature*, April 21, 1951, p. 12.

15. Mende, *Nehru*, 78; *New York Times Magazine*, September 7, 1958, pp. 13, 110.

16. Berkes and Bedi, *Diplomacy of India*, 81.

17. *Independence and After*, 246, 255; *Unity of India*, 343.

18. *India and the United Nations*, Indian Council on World Affairs, 149-50.

19. *Ibid.*, 69, 134.

20. *Nehru's Press Conferences, 1953*, pp. 35-36, 67.

21. *Nehru's Speeches, 1949-53*, p. 162; interview in *U. S. News and World Report*, September 15, 1950, p. 32; Kundra, *Indian Foreign Policy*, 133-34; *New York Times Magazine*, September 7, 1958.

22. Mende, *Nehru*, 74-76; *Nehru's Press Conferences, 1952*, p. 97.

23. *Glimpses of World History*, 812, 925; *Nehru's Speeches, 1949-53*, p. 192; *Nehru's Press Conferences, 1953*, pp. 49-50; *Vital Speeches*, December 15, 1956, p. 142.

24. *Ibid.*, December 15, 1956, p. 142; *Time*, April 11, 1955, p. 33.

25. *Independence and After*, 340; Kundra, *Indian Foreign Policy*, 88.

26. *Ibid.*, 89-92; *Nehru's Speeches, 1949-53*, p. 223.

27. *Ibid.*, 221.

28. Kundra, *Indian Foreign Policy*, 92-95.

29. *Toward Freedom*, 367-68, 387; *Unity of India*, 325; *Independence and After*, 297, 335; Levi, *Free India in Asia*, 41-42, 49, 57.

30. *Glimpses of World History*, 615-16; *Nehru's Speeches, 1949-53*, pp. 145-46.

31. *Independence and After*, 232, 250; *Nehru's Speeches, 1949-53*, p. 135.

32. *Independence and After*, 200, 217.

33. *India and the United Nations*, Indian Council on World Affairs, 30.

34. Mende, *Nehru*, 83; Murti, *Nehru's Foreign Policy*, 68-70.

35. *Nehru's Speeches, 1949-53*, p. 191. Derisive as he is of the idea of a defense at a distance, Nehru includes the Himalayan border states of Nepal, Bhutan, and Sikkim as components of India's defensive frontier.

36. *Nehru's Press Conferences, 1953*, pp. 60-61.

37. *Visit to America*, 147-48.

38. *Independence and After*, 210.

39. *Ibid.*, 242; *Nehru's Speeches, 1949-53*, p. 414; *Vital Speeches*, July 15, 1955, p. 1357; Kundra, *Indian Foreign Policy*, 62.

40. Mende, *Nehru*, 46-47, 87-88.

41. *Ibid.*, 100.

42. *Ibid.*, 63-64, 88-89.

43. *Nehru's Press Conferences, 1953*, pp. 3-4, 30.

44. Mende, *Nehru,* 81; Moraes, *Nehru,* 443; Gupta, *Indian Foreign Policy,* 66.
45. *India and the UN,* Indian Council on World Affairs, 33, 41, 69, 209-11.
46. *Ibid.,* 147-48; Kundra, *Indian Foreign Policy,* 130.
47. *Nehru's Press Conferences, 1953,* p. 64.
48. *Ibid.,* pp. 6, 11-12, 76-77; Berkes and Bedi, *Diplomacy of India,* 97.
49. *Nehru's Press Conferences, 1952,* p. 1; *Visit to America,* 135.
50. *Nehru's Speeches, 1949-53,* pp. 357-59, 362, 375.
51. *Ibid.,* 183-84.

Index